It's Just My Nonsense

The World is Full of Nonsense...
I Just Write About it.

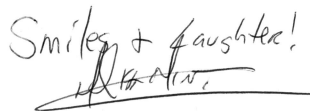

Smiles + Laughter!

MELISSA MINTZ

IT'S JUST MY NONSENSE

Disclaimer:

Published by:
Transformation Books
211 Pauline Drive #513
York, PA 17402
www.TransformationBooks.com

ISBN # 978-1-945252-08-2
Library of Congress Control No: 2016954092

Cover Design: Ranilo Cabo
Layout and typesetting: Ranilo Cabo
Editor: Michelle Cohen
Proofreader: Michelle Cohen
Midwife: Carrie Jareed

Printed in the United States of America

It's Just My Nonsense

The World is Full of Nonsense...
I Just Write About it.

You can't help getting older,
but you don't have to get old.

—*comedian George Burns (1896-1996)*

This book is dedicated to my two best friends:

My son Brandon and my daughter Morgan.

You are my inspiration. Thank you for all the fun,

the laughter, and the reminders of,

"C'mon Mom . . . just be a kid!"

PREFACE

How did this book get started?

The idea for this book started a few years ago when I was working as a pharmaceutical sales rep in Atlanta and having lunch at the office of one of my customers, Dr. Sidhu. I was an oncology clinical specialist at the time and called on mostly oncologists to educate them on our chemotherapy products.

After one of our famous Indian food lunches, where I would bring in a nice buffet of tandoori chicken, basmati rice, and some really good Indian vegetable dishes, we would discuss my products for about fifteen minutes. For the rest of the lunch hour, we would just chitchat about nothing in particular: our families, the weather, and exciting stories in the news.

We would just laugh and be silly, and I would chime in with my usual ramblings of "my nonsense" (as I always referred to it). One day after our lunch, Dr. Sidhu was laughing and she followed me out to my car while repeatedly saying, "You need to write this stuff down!" Alternating with, "When you get in the car, write this stuff down!"

I replied my usual response, "It's … just … nonsense!" Hence the title for the book: *It's Just MY Nonsense*.

As fate would have it and the synchronicity of the Universe takes place, after I left Dr. Sidhu's office I was stuck in traffic driving to my next appointment and thought, *Maybe I will write!* I didn't know what I would write about, but I grabbed a notepad and pen that was on the passenger seat, set it on my lap and started to write.

For the record, I do not recommend writing a book while you're driving around the city. As you read this book, you will understand why! Everyone who has driven with me thinks I am the worst driver ever! I need my full attention on the road. If you see me coming, you should probably move out of my way. When I started to write, it was as if I had turned on a faucet that had been blocked and the words just came gushing out. I was writing poetry and stories and anything else that came to mind.

Some of the material in this book I wrote while driving around to my physician offices. "Basket of Laundry," which is one of my favorites in the book, was written while driving through Atlanta and noticing all of the diversity in this city. I mumbled aloud, "Why can't we all just get along already?" and then I wrote "Basket of Laundry" comparing the diversity in life to the diversity of our clothes in a laundry basket. This is one of the chapters that I consider to have a subtle spiritual undertone along with the last chapter "School of Life."

I am still employed as a pharmaceutical sales rep in Atlanta; but after that lunch with Dr. Sidhu, I changed jobs and have been calling on different specialists. I have been writing on and off during that time until now, as time permits. I realize if it weren't for the suggestion to write this stuff down, I probably would not have tried writing.

For me, writing is an outlet that allows for a creative expression that I am not afforded at my technical day job of discussing pharmaceuticals and clinical studies with doctors and nurses.

In the "Introduction," I talk about restoring balance in our lives. We think of balance as right in the middle, like when we are tuning our car radios. But balance in our life is a little different; it is unique and individualized for each person. What makes one person happy may cause another person to be miserable.

How do we know when we have balance in our lives? By how we feel! Our emotions are our gauge. If you are happy and doing work you love, and have healthy loving relationships with joy and laughter, you have balance in your life. Your emotions will always let you know. If you have constant stress in your life, unhappy with the work you are doing, have difficult tumultuous relationships, then you are out of balance, and it is time to make changes to bring your life back into harmony.

When I mentioned to a few people that I was writing a book, I always referred to this as a healing book about restoring balance in your life.

For me, writing this book has helped me to create balance in my life by allowing for a creative outlet, something that I was missing from my day job, which entailed citing dosages, response rates, and side effects of the drugs that my company marketed.

No matter what else I decide to accomplish in my life, I will always think of this book as the healing book I wrote at the kitchen table. There have been many books and articles that focus on the physical benefits of laughter, but my focus is on the spiritual benefits.

I believe that through laughter and humor we can heal the world.

It's Just MY Nonsense shows you how. ...

TABLE OF CONTENTS

Disclaimer: (because every book needs one!)

If you don't like this book, there are only three people to blame:

Dr. Sidhu, my former customer, who encouraged me to "write this stuff down." Now that I think about it, maybe she was joking, but I decided I better follow doctor's orders!

My mom . . . she's not really to blame, but I am hoping that this honorable mention will guilt her into buying multiple copies for her friends, neighbors, and random people she sees at the mall.

And lastly, sometimes the editors edit out all the really good stuff. They do their best . . . really! But they can get carried away with the delete button.

Let's send them some LOVE.

Note: The author, of course, is never to blame. Ever!

INTRODUCTION

How can humor really change the world?

Humor can be used in a way to teach us to be more open and receptive to information. Have you ever wondered why most speakers start their talk with a joke or clever anecdote? It's because laughter lightens the mood. Laughter helps us to relax and be more receptive and attentive to the content being presented.

People are certainly more receptive to listening to what you have to say when they feel like they are not being lectured to. Starting a talk with humor sets the tone for a discussion for learning and sharing information in a less obtrusive way. Humor helps people to pay attention without feeling like they are being preached to.

When we incorporate humor into our conversations, we create playfulness in our discussions which help us to relate to each other in a more lighthearted way. We suddenly become less defensive and more open to listening to new ideas that we may have shunned in a more serious setting.

Humor can show us the absurdity of our actions and behaviors.

Looking at something through humor can help us to see a different viewpoint of a situation and can even help to amplify the seriousness of the issue. It does seem strange that when we look at a situation with humor, we can actually bring greater awareness to its importance. It's as if the duality of showing a serious or critical issue against the playfulness of humor can help to magnify the true nature of the issue and bring it to our attention in a new way, a way we may not have thought about before.

For instance, in the chapter "Actors," I chose to bring awareness about eating disorders. This social issue has become very destructive emotionally and physically, and in many cases life-threatening.

Our body image and beauty is now defined by our media, fashion, and entertainment industry. This is a very serious issue, but when highlighted by humor, we see a new perspective of how starving ourselves intentionally just seems absurd and completely ridiculous. This is because we can use humor to see the same situation differently from a new point of view. Since our perspective has changed, what we believe about the situation has changed. Humor can show us a new perspective.

Through humor we can show an exaggerated view of an issue that can make it seem absurd. We can now see the same situation in a new reality, which could finally inspire us to make a positive change.

On several topics in this book, I chose to write from a more lighthearted perspective when discussing several specific issues that we share collectively to allow the issue to come to light. Some of the issues that we are currently dealing with are: violence in "Prison Break," bigotry and racism in "Basket of Laundry," eating disorders in "Actors," and planetary destruction in "Pretty Toilet." We have been dealing with the same problems now for many decades.

"Prison Break" heightens awareness of the violence that has been interspersed into the entertainment industry in feature films, television, and video games. It is important to bring attention to this issue; if we want a more peaceful society, why are we constantly introducing violence?

It's as if we have become desensitized to violence by viewing so much of it as entertainment, we are unable to discern what is real and what is staged for our own amusement. There have been images in the televised news of people who are being victimized and passersby just ignoring them. Has all the violence displayed in our media desensitized us so much that we have become an uncaring, apathetic society?

"Basket of Laundry" shows us that we really are much more alike than we are different. What we judge our differences on—our outer appearance—is really just an illusion. If we all continue to see only our differences, we will continue to have strife and discord on the planet. It is only when we realize how similar we really are that we will finally be able to live in a world of peace and harmony.

"Pretty Toilet" depicts the immense beauty of our planet—our oceans. This is the home of two thirds of our planet—aquatic life. The plant and animal life are allowing us into their home to frolic and enjoy! Unfortunately, we have become nightmare guests. It's as if we walk into their home and say, "Gosh, I love what you've done with the place!" Then we just trash the house and don't bother to clean up after ourselves.

If we had house guests like that we certainly wouldn't invite them back. We have become unwanted visitors in the home of our aquatic friends. By destroying their home, we are destroying our home as well: the planet Earth.

Unless we change our actions of how we view each other and our world, we will still be dealing with the same issues tomorrow that we are dealing with today. How will our tomorrows be different from today? By consciously making a change.

If we want to change our world, we need to make changes in our world.

These changes in our world start with each individual mind—changing how we think! Have you ever been in a classroom where you did not understand the material that was discussed, then a friend or a classmate explained something a little differently and then you just got it? This is what we can accomplish through humor—to explain something a little differently in a new way that can help people finally take notice.

Humor can be used in a way to change our perspective—to help us see a situation in a new light.

When we change our perspective, we change our viewpoint.
When we change our viewpoint, we change our thoughts.
When we change our thoughts, we change what we believe.
When we change what we believe, we can change the world.

Our new beliefs about ourselves and the world can change our life, and we can do this while laughing. With our new awareness, we are able to take action together and create global change on our planet. Once we realize the global issues that we face collectively, we will take action to change our beliefs and work together as a unified force. Only with this *unity of consciousness* can we change our lives and our world from planetary destruction, which was a result of our lack of reverence, carelessness, and disregard for our earthly home.

By changing our perspective through humor, we may see a situation from a different vantage point and finally realize that now is the time to do something. How many times have you heard someone say about a crisis, "Gosh! That's terrible! I wish somebody would do something about that!" Well, we are that somebody. We are who we have been waiting for!!! It is us—all of us! Let's stop waiting for someone else. Who else is there?

Each and every one of us has a responsibility to maintain and take care of our home. It's no different than family members all pitching in to make sure the house they live in is clean and properly maintained so decay and destruction won't ensue.

5

Humor can show us that we are a lot more alike than we realize.

Why do we take ourselves so seriously all of the time? The things all of us do are funny and goofy. Are we really that much different? We laugh at the experiences and situations in life that we can relate to. Have you even been to a comedy club with a group of your friends and after the comedian said something you laughed, elbowed your friend, and said, "I've thought about that before, too" or "I had a similar thing happen to me"? In this book, I talk about the experiences that I am having during this time in my life. I'm sure they are very similar experiences and conversations other people are having in their own lives. Many of us seem to think that our experiences and situations are unique only to us. When we realize our experiences are actually shared with others, we tend to feel a greater connection with the people in our lives.

Laughter brings people together. When we laugh, we all speak the same language. Everyone understands laughter. Laughter is universal.

Humor can help us shift the focus from our differences to our similarities.

We laugh because we can see how similar our experiences really are. I'm sure I am not the only one who has thought, *Why are we blessing the people who sneeze all over us?* (chapter 3, "Bless You") Just doesn't seem right, huh? But we do it! We think we are being polite and socially conscious! We just seem to follow what other people do, even if we don't know why. We may have heard someone do something or say something and decided to incorporate this behavior into our lives just . . . because.

People are funny. Isn't that why we all love to sit down, relax and people watch. We love to watch what other people do and see how they live their lives. This is why the reality television shows have become so popular.

We have become so addicted to watching how other people live their lives because we realize their families are just as dysfunctional as ours are! It has been somewhat of a pleasant validation to know that other families yell and scream at each other too, and have problems just like the rest of us. If we only see our differences, we will continue to live in a reality that is separate from each other with disharmony and constant conflict. It is only when we realize how alike we really are that we will finally have unity and peace.

Unity is Peace.

Laughter is a conductor of peace; when we are laughing we can't be fighting. When we all stop bickering and hating each other for our perceived differences based on skin color, religion, and our culture differences, we will finally live in harmony.

Humor reminds us to be more childlike.

Research has shown that children laugh at least 300 times a day, whereas adults laugh about 15 times a day. Children laugh just for the joy of laughter because they experience joy over the simplest of things. Adults usually need a reason to laugh.

In the last chapter "School of Life," I talk about being more childlike in how we relate to our world. When we were kids we didn't constantly worry about life. We were carefree and lived in the moment. As we got older we learned to take things more seriously, suppress our laughter, and act like grownups, or at least our idea of what we thought a grownup was supposed to be like. We worried more ... about our jobs, our families, paying the bills, our health, and just about everything else. Life became associated with constant stress and stressful situations. This constant stress has destroyed our relationships with family and friends, and it destroyed our health.

Humor helps restore the balance in our lives, which creates more joy.

Generally speaking, the people who have laughter, joy, and love in their lives are not the ones who are getting sick. The majority of all illness is caused by stress and how we react to stressful situations. Constant stress decreases our immune function and creates a caustic environment both physically and emotionally. When we are run down due to stress, we are prone to illness and disease.

With all the demands of life, many of us have become emotionally drained and physically lethargic as we move through each day in a robotic perfunctory existence. We may feel like we have too many things on our plate as we try to cope with the stress in our jobs, our relationships, and financial issues. Laughter is a wonderful stress buster. Laughter instantly reduces stress and tension. Have you ever been in a room full of people and someone made a funny or silly comment, and people laughed? Even if it was for only a brief moment, do you remember what a tension reliever that moment was?

From that moment in time moving forward, the people in the group seemed more relaxed and less anxious. It's as if you could feel the tension in the room immediately dissipate to be replaced with a more relaxed atmosphere.

We have all experienced the benefits of laughter. Remember those times when you were in a bad mood, then a friend or coworker said something that made you laugh and your whole outlook immediately changed? Instead of an attitude of sadness and gloom, you suddenly became more joyful and optimistic about the rest of your day. Laughter can change our mental outlook very quickly. Isn't this why we enjoy being around people who can make us laugh?

Laughter helps us to release negative feelings and emotions that we may have accumulated during the day. Have you ever laughed so hard you felt like you needed a nap? Laughter helps us feel lighter and happier. When we laugh we are completely in the present. We are not thinking about the past; we are not worried about the future. We are completely in the **now.** We are just enjoying the moment.

Did you know that when we laugh we raise our vibration and attract to us more of what we want in life? Joy attracts more joy and joyful experiences.

May this book be a gentle reminder to restore the balance in your life, to be less serious, to have more FUN, and to LAUGH!

So, go ahead and LAUGH—even if you have no reason.

I hope you enjoy reading this book as much as I enjoyed writing it. What was I doing while I was writing this book? I laughed ... and laughed ... and laughed a little more.

Smiles and Laughter,

Melissa

1

Diary of a Drug Rep

Have you ever seen a lady in two-inch heels chasing your doctor down the hallway? Well ... that would be me. Glad we could finally meet!

I am a pharmaceutical sales rep. Drug rep, as the doctors' offices refer to us. I get paid to sell drugs. My job is to talk to the doctors in the offices and convince them to prescribe my company's drugs for their patients. I have to admit, I like my job, most days anyhow, but it seems like the strangest job. Even while I am doing the job, I think it's kind of weird. I spend my days driving around listening to the radio, carrying in food for lunch, and sitting in the waiting room or leaning against the wall in the hallway near the exam room.

I lean and wait to get a glimpse of the doctor for the required signature for the samples I am leaving. Each of these *lean and wait* times can be thirty minutes or more. It seems the doctors depend on us to be there to decorate their walls. As you know, paintings can be expensive!

"I have always wanted to do that!" I can't even remember how many times I have heard someone say this. Many people have the impression that it is a very glamorous job. After all, it seems very glamorous; we drive a nice car (usually a company car); we have a salary and quarterly bonus; and we call on highly-educated professionals—or as they would say in the South—really smart people. And the best part is that we do not report to an office. We each have an assigned territory for the doctors that we call on.

There are days I may spend a total of five minutes actually having a conversation with a doctor. Most days they only have enough time to sign for the drug samples as they are rushing down the hallway from one exam room to the next. The tall brunette running after them is me, pleading for thirty seconds of their time. See, the way it works is, selling requires talking, even if it's to the back of their fast-moving head.

Do I really need a college degree to cater in lunch and lean against a wall? This is the question I ask myself every day. My initial response, of course, is *NO*. But then, after careful consideration, I realize only a highly-educated professional like myself could decide—baked chicken or pot roast.

"Hi, Melissa," I hear Tammy, the office manager, say, and I turn around to face her so that my other shoulder now leans against the wall. "Dr. Butts is in with a new patient, Melissa, so he won't be out for another thirty minutes. Why don't you just schedule a lunch?"

A free lunch for these offices is a really big deal. These lunches can make or break your career. The offices expect us to bring them in lunch and many schedule drug rep lunches every single day. I, along with the other reps, comply to this request in the hopes of getting more selling time with the doctor. On many occasions though, we just get more time with the office staff; sometimes we see the doctors and sometimes we don't.

I walk over to the window where Tammy is sitting to schedule the lunch. "What would y'all like to eat?" I casually ask.

"Well," Tammy continues, "if you don't bring us in what we want to eat, the doctor may never see you again. It has happened before. It could happen to you."

"Oh my gosh. That's just horrible!" I say as if somebody just got mugged or hit by a car. *Ugh! Here we go again,* I thought, *another lunch threat.* I have even resorted to removing my home address from my business cards for fear of lunch retribution.

"I'll make sure I don't bring in a bad lunch. What would you like?" I ask nervously while taking copious notes.

"The doctor would like barbecue ribs, macaroni and cheese, fried okra, and some cornbread. Oh yeah, make sure you bring the banana pudding with the vanilla wafers and the whipped cream on top. That's what the doctor likes, so bring a lot!"

"Is that it?" I say as sweetly as possible only by rationalizing all this with, *Well my company pays not me! Looks like I'll be eating some good barbecue on Thursday!*

"Don't forget the sweet tea!!!" Tammy yells at my back as I am halfway out the door.

"Yeah, right!" I say, berating myself while walking back to my car. "The doctor wants this . . . the doctor wants that. What a bunch of food whores!" The office staff could care less what the doctor wants. It just sounds better than, "Tammy wants a slab of ribs."

I drive over to my next appointment to see Dr. Patel. *Thank goodness I have an appointment,* I thought, as I bop my head from side to side singing to "Fireflies" by Owl City on the radio.

"Hi Jessie!" I yell over and wave to the receptionist as I walk in.

"Oh Melissa, we tried to call you this morning."

"Why? What's going on, Jessie? Did Dr. Patel have to run over to the hospital?"

"Oh no . . . nothing like that," she says while waving her hand to dismiss the notion. "It's about the lunch you brought in last week," she continued.

"Oh, the chili and baked potato bar with all the toppings? Was everything okay?" I asked, realizing it's not even ten in the morning yet and I am already in the midst of another food war.

"It was really good and all. Well, the girls and I were talking, and we were really craving chocolate."

"But I brought in brownies for dessert! Remember?" I didn't want to sound defensive, so I added, "The assorted brownies weren't good?"

"No, Melissa. It's not that. The reason why I was going to call you is because we were really craving chocolate cake. Next time bring in a whole chocolate cake!"

I guess they just gave me their lunch order for Friday, I realized. Then I grabbed a boring *Golf* magazine from the table and found a spot against the wall to wait for the doctor.

As I said earlier, I think my job is a little weird, but I also think my customers are weird, too. Now, I don't mean this in a mean-spirited way. I don't think they are weird as people per se. I just think it is weird to refer to doctors as Dr. Jones or Dr. Smith. Why is it that we have to refer to our physician as doctor so and so?

It is a major social faux pas to even consider calling the doctor by his/her first name. I have never understood this! I have been employed by billion dollar companies, and we were always on a first name basis with everyone, including the CEO. There was no, "Hi, Mr. or Mrs. So and So." But if you are a doctor, society puts you on such a high pedestal that you are simply above the mere mortal.

Somehow medical school changes a human from being a mere mortal to a M.inor D.iety. This is why when a student graduates from medical school they are now able to sign their name with an M.D. after it. This is a requirement to show the transformation of the human to superhuman status at the completion of medical school.

After all, could we really believe that someone just like ourselves could help us get better when we are sick? We have created this illusion that someone with a greater power now determines our fate—do we live or do we die.

I want a white coat, too!!! This is their cloak of magical powers! As soon as the white coat is put on we are forbidden to address the doctor by their first name. We are not deemed worthy. We didn't put in the time in medical school. We didn't dissect dead people in the cadaver lab. We didn't stay awake for forty-eight grueling hours at a time doing hospital rounds.

As soon as the magical white coat is worn, it's no longer Dave or John ... Larry or Tom ... Sue or Mary ... Nancy or Keri. *"My name is Doctor with a capital D."*

My mom seems to think that when a person graduates from medical school they are now an authoritative figure on every single topic. It does not matter if the question is not medically related. "He's a doctor ... he knows!" is my mom's favorite response whenever I ask her why she runs most of her decisions past my brother.

"Why are you asking Larry a financial question? He doesn't know anything about your taxes!"

"He's a doctor; he should know this!" my mom replies as if I am clueless about the magical power of the white coat. "I'm also going to call him about the spot on my leg to see if he can tell me what it is over the phone."

"But Mom ... he's a pediatrician. Do you have the chicken pox?" I asked, hoping she could see how ridiculous this idea was. "Why don't you go in person to see a real doctor; it could be serious! He treats babies and little kids," I continued, trying to talk her out of a phone consult with my brother Larry—the pediatrician. "You should see a dermatologist! I'm a drug rep!" I say as convincingly as possible. "You really need to see a dermatologist and have some tissue removed and sent to the lab."

While I was saying this, I wished I had on a white coat to give me some scientific credibility. Without the magical cloak, I was only a regular human—just a daughter who worked as a sales rep. I realize that trying to reason with my mom is like trying to get my dog to poop outside on a rainy day. It's not going to happen!

I really don't understand this professional hierarchy that we have created in our society. I know that "doctor" trumps "drug rep." Okay, that's really obvious for two reasons. First, doctors have a food group named after them (yes, apparently so—soda is now considered a food group). Second, they call me Melissa; and I, in turn, call them Doctor.

Does published author trump doctor? Will my mom then call me with a financial question, too?! Will she say when talking to her friends, "She's an author . . . she knows!" Or will my brother, the doctor, still be the family favorite?

After spending twelve years as a drug rep, I changed jobs and was starting with a new company calling on different specialists. Instead of calling on oncologists, I was calling on gastroenterologists with a drug for Crohn's disease, which affects the bowel.

I decided I would do a little experiment. I wanted to see if I called all of my doctors by their first name whether or not they would become offended and correct me. The very first day I started working in my territory I decided to put my little experiment to work. I called every doctor by their first name and introduced myself as their new drug rep.

Not one doctor corrected me, seemed offended, or asked me to address them as Doctor. The only people who seemed offended and corrected me were the nurses, who would interject, "You mean Dr. Jones . . . not Tom." I realized I should still refer to them as Doctor to the staff. After all, the nurses and the front office staff did not know of my little experiment, and I didn't want to seem disrespectful to them.

After the second week of my experiment, I had several of my physicians call me at home just to talk. These were personal calls about office politics or wanting to get on my speakers' list. I also had several physicians call and invite me to socialize with them and their families. It seemed that since I did not create this separation of doctor/drug rep, they treated me like a peer, a friend actually. It was no longer necessary for the doctor to try and live up to this societal expectation of the all-knowing authoritative healer. When I called them by their first name, just as they referred to me, we were more like colleagues.

There was no title to suggest a division of status. It was how complete strangers who met on a daily walk or at their kids' baseball game would greet each other, just two people having a conversation. I could not keep up with all the personal calls and social invitations, and by the time I started with my next company, I decided to go back to calling every physician by his/her real first name: Doctor.

Our society has put doctors on such a high pedestal that they even have their own soft drink named after them: Dr. Pepper. I have always wondered what his specialty was. Any relation to Miss Salt on my kitchen table? Could this be his wife? I just wonder . . . salt and pepper sounds so right together. Miss Salt and Dr. Pepper . . . nice ring to it. Those two should definitely be married!

Could Mr. Pibb be their son? Is he in medical school? Get ready, y'all, Dr. Pibb will be on the store shelves very soon. I hear he is being held back a year due to difficulty in the cadaver lab. Something about sticky hands and holding the scalpel. Makes you wonder how Dr. Pepper got through it. Those silly sodas with their sugary sticky hands! Really! How do they manage?

We don't drink any other profession! Just not good enough I guess. There's no drug rep cola at my grocery store. No wonder my mom doesn't listen to me. I have picked an unworthy profession! There is no food group named after drug reps. It's a shame, really. We spend so much of our time bringing in goodies and meals to the doctor's office with all the lunches, cookies, and cakes, the food industry can't just throw us a bone and name a little soft drink after us?

No matter what profession we have, we all share one thing in common. We wait . . . and wait . . . and wait . . . to see the doctor.

Didn't you ever wonder why you had to wait so long to see your doctor? Most people think it's because they schedule their patient appointments too close together and get behind early in the day. By late afternoon, the wait time can be up to two hours or more. When you do finally get back into the exam room, your actual time with the doctor is only about ten minutes.

I can definitely tell you from years of experience of calling on doctors that patient scheduling issues are not the real reason for the long wait. There is a very good reason and I have kept this a secret long enough. Now is the time to share this information with all of you wondering people.

But first, let's be realistic here. There are not very many professionals we would wait more than two hours to see. If I have an appointment with my daughter's teacher and I had to wait more than an hour, I guarantee you I would leave. I had an appointment. Isn't my time valuable, too? Certainly my time is as valuable as the teacher's. Do you really think I would still be sitting on the little bench in the school office waiting for two hours? "Oh ... Miss Teacher ... Miss Teacher! I'm still sitting here. Do you think you will still come out and talk to me for ten minutes?"

I can't think of very many situations where I would wait for hours to talk with someone for ten minutes. If I was at a store, standing in line for the cashier, I would not wait in line for two hours. After what I considered to be a reasonable amount of time, which for me is about twenty minutes tops, I would put the merchandise down and leave.

I would not even wait two hours to ride Space Mountain at Disneyland. If I was in a restaurant and two hours had passed, and I did not have my food, not only would I leave, but before I did I would make sure I got a voucher for a free meal for myself and the kids!

I think my hairdresser is very creative. I like going to her to get a haircut, but if I was waiting for an hour … see ya!

We will wait … and wait … and wait … till it is our turn to see the doctor. We'll just sit there and wait and read those outdated magazines from 1998-2002, *Field & Stream, Family Circle, Redbook, Business Week, Sports Illustrated*, and of course, the ubiquitous *Golf* magazine. The really good magazines that are current from this time period like *People, Us Weekly,* and *Entertainment* have already been taken home by the disgruntled patients before you.

The doctors know we are guaranteed a long wait, so why don't they make the experience a little more enjoyable? After all, aren't we the customers? What happened to good service and taking care of the customers?

We are paying them to provide a service. We came to see them, not the other way around. The least doctors could do is be a little more affable. When was the last time a doctor thanked you for coming into their business? Any other business, when I purchase something or pay for a service, they thank *me*. Why? It's because I am the customer.

We are the patrons. Let's not forget about this important fact. We should expect and demand better service. They don't even bother to give out cards for frequent visit discounts. Even when I buy a smoothie, after the tenth visit I get one for free.

The offices should be a fun place to spend time. If they were, you wouldn't have so many people dreading to see their doctor. The waiting room could be turned into a little movie theater with surround sound, of course, for that intimate home theater feel. There could be a small screen with a couple rows of stadium seating for a better view. A self-service popcorn machine is always a good idea, since we will most likely have enough time to watch the entire movie.

If the waiting room is large enough, what about a pool table? We could mingle with the other patients and play a game of pool to pass the time. We could have teams and play against each other. Anything has to be better than all of the patients just staring at each other for two hours trying to figure out why each one is there. That's what I do to pass the time. "Let's see, did they cough or sneeze . . . nope . . . probably not respiratory then. I don't see any limping or hurt appendages—no blood anywhere. Oh well, I've got another couple of hours to figure it all out."

So, for all my friends who have been waiting on the secret of the long boring hours in the waiting room devoid of any type of fun and entertainment, well, you don't have to wonder anymore! I have the answer. It's finally time to divulge this clandestine information that has been hidden from the public far too long.

Are you ready? The real reason why we have to wait for hours and hours to get a few minutes of our doctor's time: It's the *Revenge of the Nerds*.

DIARY OF A DRUG REP

This is true! Remember all of those guys and girls in high school that everyone thought were the nerdy brainiacs, the kids who were a little odd and nobody could relate to?

The nerds who got an A+ in science class, participated and placed in the science fair, volunteered their free time as the math tutors, and were always the first ones finished dissecting the formaldehyde frog?

Do you remember the kids that no one picked in gym class? The same kids who preferred chemistry lab over team sports?

The guys who gave up football and baseball to spend time studying after school, preparing for their future? The girls who didn't bother with cheerleading? Friday night football games were out. This was study time!

Remember the really smart girls who were in all the honors math and science classes, who traded popularity for honor roll?

For all of you out there who made fun of the science geeks and the non-athletes in high school, well, this is their revenge on all you people!

The science geeks and the gym class flunkies are now our doctors. Yes! . . . and they are getting their revenge!!!

These kids are all grown up now, but they still remember how everyone thought they were freaks and nerds in high school. They remember how the other kids teased them, only to later beg to copy their homework and cheat off their tests. So now these former nerds have achieved hierarchy in our society. Their title alone is associated with money, power, and magical superhuman ability. Instead of diplomatic immunity they have doctor immunity for the rest of their lives!

They can make you wait two hours to see them, never show up for an appointment, never return phone calls, and it's acceptable!

They can just say, "I'm sorry, but I was busy saving a life." And this is from a dermatologist!

2

Airport Security

Do you remember the good ole days? The days when penny candy was really a penny. When kids used to run and play outdoors and climb the trees. When we could figure out how to use our simple electronic gadgets without reading directions. When gas stations actually pumped your gas and washed your windshields. When an entire family could go to the movies for under ten dollars.

These certainly were the good ole days and I miss them, too. But this wasn't really what I was referring to. Nowadays when I reminisce about the good ole days, I'm referring to airport security.

How I miss the days when we walked through the metal detector fully dressed and if the alarm didn't sound we were good to go. The days where my bottled water that quenched my nirst was not considered a possible liquid explosive. I miss the times when my friends and family could walk to the gate with me, hang out and talk until I boarded the plane. These are the memories that bring back those nostalgic wistful yearnings of days gone by, the memories that bring a smile to my happy face.

"Where o' where has my simple world gone?" I find myself silently repeating this mantra every time I go to the airport. Back in the day, I used to love to travel. I couldn't wait to go to the airport and fly off to some exotic vacation destination. I was happy just to go anywhere really, even if it meant only a change of scenery in some small remote town or being holed up in an airport hotel for a business meeting.

Traveling used to be fun and exciting. Now I associate traveling with another one of my least favorite things to do—moving! I have always heard people say, "Moving is the biggest pain!" Now people say this about airport security.

Traveling on an airplane is becoming more difficult every day. Just to get through security has become such a big ordeal! *Why did I bother to get dressed this morning?* I hear my own voice screaming inside my head as I proceed to take my bin like a good little traveler who knows the rules. As I am standing in the long line awaiting my turn to walk through the metal detector, I find myself wondering if my socks have any embarrassing holes in them. Will my pants stay up okay when I take off my belt? *Is my boss behind me?* I silently ask myself, not wanting to look. *I think I have on one black sock and one blue sock, and I don't want to take off my blazer now! I'm wearing a really skimpy spaghetti strap tank top! This is so embarrassing!!*

Normally, I wouldn't really care; but since I am traveling to my company's national sales meeting, I wish I would have thought these things out to make sure there would be no embarrassing moments when traveling with coworkers.

I start my performance for the required security striptease. Off with my shoes, my belt, my blazer, my jewelry, and carefully placing my clothing in the bin to be scrutinized for weapon control. I await the hand wave directing me to walk the line through the detector and scramble to find my clothes and get dressed for the second time that day. Why am I stripping for free? I could use those dollar bills to repurchase the bottled water that was thrown out during my security check!

Eventually, I think we will all be going through airport security in our underwear. Why bother to get dressed at all in the mornings before we travel to the airport? Where are the *snuggies* when you need 'em? I used to make fun of those things. The silly commercials of people sitting in bleachers watching their kids' sporting events wearing their color-of-choice blanket with sleeves. When my kids would start acting up, I would use this to threaten them. "If you don't behave, I'm going to your basketball game wearing a snuggie!"

"Morgan, if you don't clean your room, I'll watch you cheer at the next football game in a snuggie!" I thought this was the purpose of the snuggie—to threaten your children with the fear of embarrassment if you wear this blanket muumuu while in their presence in a public place.

I think I may have just discovered a new universal legitimate use for the snuggie. Why don't they just sell a lightweight airport snuggie that we wear for traveling? We would all be dressed alike so no one would feel underdressed and out of place. It would be like the traveler's uniform: snuggie and bare feet. Just think how quickly security lines would move if passengers didn't have to take off any articles of clothing.

And the best part is we would already have a blanket for the freezing cold airplane. I am one of those people that is always cold when I travel on those darn planes. If it's ninety degrees outside in the summer, I look like I'm traveling to Minnesota in the winter. They do have heat on the plane. So why can't the plane's interior be at a comfortable temperature? There are rarely enough blankets to go around. The airplane blankets are disgustingly gross anyhow. These communal blankets shed more hair than my dog from being used and reused.

If you think you are getting a clean blanket because you take off the plastic wrapping—think again. Chances are your blanket has already been used from flight to flight and rewrapped to look freshly cleaned. Y'know what Tiger Woods and your airline blanket have in common? They have both been sleeping around a bit too much. It doesn't matter though, does it? We are wearing our warm, comfortable, airline-approved, FAA regulated, multi-functional, traveling muumuu snuggie.

What amazes me is that we have all of this security before we get on the plane and virtually no security once we actually board the airplane. Our security guards on the plane are the flight attendants. Let's face it—their main concern is bringing us our drinks and peanuts before the end of the flight.

The flight attendants are not adequately trained to deal with an unruly passenger! This is why when a passenger is acting loony on the airplane they just duct tape them to their seat and hand them over to the police when they land.

There were two stories in the news recently about passengers who were being unruly and were duct taped to their seat. One is about a guy who was drinking and was verbally abusive. This probably wasn't a very big deal. In his inebriated state, the guy probably thought the flight attendants were just playing some kind of sexy drinking game. "Hey there, big boy! I'm gonna tie you up so I can have my way with you while we fly through the friendly skies. Up ... Up ... and away. ... "

The other story is about a woman who slapped a flight attendant on the butt, then fell over on top of a blind passenger. Obviously, the blind passenger did not see the crazy, ass-smackin' lady falling, or most likely would have moved out of her way. Evidently, airline policy states that only pilots can spank the flight attendants.

Duct tape used to be the silver tape I would buy at Home Depot to tape on my ventilation duct when I bought a new clothes dryer. I never even knew it was a weapon. I didn't have to apply for a duct tape permit or show any type of identification. They don't know I'm not a flight attendant! Why didn't the cashier ask for some type of airline ID badge?

You think the passengers are able to help in an emergency situation? After the initial boarding where we all glance around at the other passengers to play a head game of

Who's the Terrorist, we go back to reading our magazines, listening to our iPods, or working on our computers. Most passengers are totally oblivious to anything that is happening on the airplane!

I travel quite a bit on business trips and personal travel, and I can tell you there are three huge onboard security issues that need to be addressed immediately, not only for passenger safety, but for our sanity as well.

The #1 SECURITY issue ON the airplane is "passenger seat hog!"

I can't even tell you how many times I have sat down in my seat and the person sitting next to me lifts up the arm rest right before they sit so they can have more room! I paid for a full seat!!! All of a sudden, I am sharing my seat with a total stranger who now has half of my seat and all of his. I can't think of any other situation where a complete stranger would sit down in my seat without even asking permission!

Why don't the flight attendants duct tape the passengers butt cheeks together so I can have my own seat! That'll prevent the spillage into the adjacent seat! The arm rest is there for a reason. It's not there just to rest your arm on; it's also a seat divider. When it stays down, I have a secured full seat. All of that space is mine.

"Heelloooo! We do have individual seats! Does your ticket say row 16?" This, of course, is what I would like to say to my seat-hogging seatmate. Why can't the passengers be a little more courteous? I would appreciate some compensation for unwillingly having to give up my seat. How about, "Excuse me, ma'am. I could really use more space than my seat allows. Could I pay you for half of your seat? I brought cash!"

I am now squished in my new airplane love seat for two. My ribs are being crammed against the single arm rest that is still down and the other side is sitting cheek to cheek with my new unwanted plane friend whose big butt is a little too close to mine! The seats keep getting smaller and the butts keep getting bigger. It's time to accommodate all of the expanding passengers and add another seating section: first class, coach, economy and wide booty.

The worst experience is the dreaded middle seat flights where my seatmates on both sides lift up the arm rest and plop down. Barely able to breathe, I become compressed like a squished marshmallow allowed only to expand in the small remaining space that is left sandwiched between them. *If I were in a s'more I would have more room than this!*

The airplanes should have a few wide booty rows in the back of the plane with no arm rests! If your boarding ticket says row 48, you'll know why you're there, and I may actually have a more comfortable flight. I have been to movie theaters that have the moveable arm rests, and I have never had a complete stranger lift up the armrest and squish their butt up against mine!

There seem to be no rules for airplane etiquette at all! I have even had passengers sitting next to me steal my air vent. There always seems to be one idiot who has all the air vents turned toward them. Once you're on the plane, all of the nice amenities become a free-for-all.

These are probably the same people who try to steal the tissue and toilet paper from the airplane bathroom. *I paid enough for my seat. All this is mine ... mine ... mine!* You know who you are—the people who rearrange the over-head compartment above their seat to move their neighbors' items to another location so that you won't be inconvenienced.

The #2 SECURITY issue ON the airplane is "Fart Finder."

This is some new security jargon that is used for all major airlines. It is a technical term for "Who the heck farted?" There's nothing worse than being stuck in my airplane loveseat and the person sitting next to me lets out a silent but deadly killer. I think the only reason for its actual silence is due to the loud buzz of the airplane's engine.

Airplanes have recycled air. We are all breathing the same air for the entire duration of the flight. The fart has nowhere to go! The smelly fart seems to keep ricocheting off the airplane walls. The smell goes away, then five minutes later it bounces off the seat in front of me, and I have to smell it again. We cannot roll down the windows like we would if we were driving in our cars. We have to smell the fart for the entire trip. There's just nowhere for it to go!

Farting is the new yawn. Y'know how when you see other people yawn you feel like you have to yawn, too. Well, on an airplane, when a few of the passengers start to smell the fart, they seem to feel like they need to fart, too!

What are the flight attendants doing to protect the re-circulated air? Find the farters!!! They have banned cigarettes so we can breathe cleaner air, so why should I have to smell a fart for five hours. Due to the lack of fresh air to dilute the contained fart, I start trying to figure out what the person just ate. *Let's see, smells like a cheeseburger with onion, and there's definitely a hint of garlic. Hmmmmmm. I think I kinda smell some ice cream–possibly a chocolate malt.* If you're a frequent flyer, you too could be a fart connoisseur. It's akin to describing a fine wine. You eventually develop a nose for it and become more proficient with practice.

I have had enough of this. I press the button for the flight attendant, who finally sees my light on after she strolls down the aisle from the back of the plane. Apparently, flirting with the cute guy in seat 37C for the last hour was more important to her than my comfort and safety.

Is this the new sky dating? Find a guy you like on an airplane and chat them up for the duration of the flight while they are strapped in their seat. It's not like they can go anywhere!

"Hey, Miss Fight Attendant! We need more duct tape! Didn't you see my light on? I pressed the button a while ago. I've had to smell this fart for two hours already! Could you please tape this guy's butt together! No ... not him ... the one sitting next to me in my loveseat! All those bags of peanuts are making the passengers fart!"

All of these things are a breach of security! There's no one on the airplane to protect us. What are we going to do, throw a peanut at them?

I am really surprised that the flight attendants are still serving peanuts as a snack aboard the plane. There have been recent reports of salmonella and continuing reports of the growing number of people who develop severe peanut allergies.

According to airline policy, I can eat the *death snack,* but I can't bring a tube of toothpaste in my carry-on if the tube is bigger than three ounces. Peanuts have killed more people than my toothpaste. I am tired of packing the little tubes—they only last for a part of my vacation. I brush my teeth after every meal! Why am I penalized for good dental hygiene?

Remember when peanuts were banned from the airplanes and they started giving out the snack size bag of pretzels. As it turns out, more people prefer peanuts over pretzels. The passengers got used to the fart smell, so the nuts won—and they're back.

For the three million Americans allergic to peanuts, *The Return of the Nuts* sounds like a really bad horror movie. Passengers are still battling over the peanut/pretzel debate. Why is this such a difficult dilemma? If people are still fighting over peanuts and pretzels, don't serve either. How about popcorn? Who doesn't love a good bag of popcorn! I have never met anyone who is allergic to popcorn; it's just un-American!

Now most of the airplanes have a television on the back of the seat, so popcorn is a required food. It's almost like a "food law" or something. That's why all movie theaters serve popcorn. If you have ever seen a police officer in a movie theater lobby, that's why—to enforce the popcorn law.

They should just put one of those large movie theater popcorn machines in the back of the plane. Popcorn is inexpensive and only takes a few minutes to pop. The flight attendants could walk up and down the aisle carrying the hot melted butter on their carts.

Who eats peanuts with television?! Are we at a baseball game? We shouldn't be arguing over peanuts or pretzels ... We should be arguing over buttered or not buttered! This is the question the flight attendants should be asking.

The #3 SECURITY issue ON the airplane is "passenger prattle!"

This is airplane jargon for passengers who won't shut up! They talk and talk about every stupid, inconsequential, and boring detail of their life.

I have had passengers who have sat down next to me and told me the most intimate details of their life. "Oh, hello ... I'm flying back home from a convention. I had a really great time! I drank too much and slept with one of my coworkers after the awards night—feel a little guilty. But I'm just really stressed because I'm close to being fired, and we just found out my daughter is pregnant and plans on dropping out of high school with her loser, druggie dropout boyfriend of six weeks."

It doesn't matter that I do not even have a chance to respond to the "Hello." These people know that you are strapped in; there is nowhere to move, since almost all flights are now overbooked. The only empty seat you can find on a plane anymore is the toilet, and that seat is not even empty for very long.

It's those darn peanuts again! They're the culprit! The peanuts are also a laxative. Apparently, the oil from the nuts helps things to move. If the passenger sitting next to you asks for an extra bag, you can be guaranteed a smelly, farty flight! I guess there's nothing like a really good poop 26,000 feet up in the sky. It's probably a good thing; nobody wants to be constipated when having an anaphylaxis reaction to the nuts. That would just be misery times two!

Whether we like it or not, we become a therapist in the sky. This is free therapy! We have to sit there and take it. These *loquacious Lucy's and Lenny's* just press their recline button, lie back in a comfortable position in their makeshift couch, and start their prating to the astounded passenger strapped in the seat next to them.

They know we can't escape!!! They certainly would not want to burden their friends or family with their issues; only a complete stranger who has nowhere to go will suffice. Sure, I have tried the many different tactics: reading a book; working on my computer; wearing headphones— it does not work! These *patients* know you can still hear them!

I think the rationale must be that a person thinks, *I'll never see this passenger again. I have not even divulged my real name. I can say whatever I want, and it will never come back to me.* I always wondered what O.J. Simpson said to his seatmate when he flew from Los Angeles to Chicago for the Hertz convention on the evening of the alleged double murder on June 12, 1994. Did the conversation start with, "Hello ... if I did it. ... "

"If I did it, this is how I would have killed my ex-wife and her boyfriend. If I did it, I would have made sure I did it really quickly so it would look like I didn't have time before my flight. I'm telling you this ... if I did it ... because I didn't. I couldn't have committed the murder; the glove I wore was too tight and didn't fit well! I would have worn better-fitting gloves!

"I may even write a book one day explaining how I did it, that is, if I did it. I might just call it *If I Did It*. Has a nice ring to it. Don't you think so, Charlie? ... or ... whatever your name is."

Our flight attendants are the people in control. They are like our SWAT team in the sky. We depend on them for our safety and protection. The flight attendants are armed with duct tape and have complete access to the microphone. Pick up the microphone and take charge! "Hey, prattle-face in 16C! It's time to shut up! We had a complaint from the lady sharing your loveseat. It's time to shut up and stop farting ... Okay, buddy?

"I'd hate to have to come over there and duct tape your mouth, dude! I have a brand new roll!

"Let's just stop the talking and nobody will get hurt."

Isn't this the kind of service we all expect and are paying for? After all, airline tickets keep going up and they aren't even serving those free mystery meat sandwiches anymore on those big stale rolls. We are paying for our new duct tape armed SWAT team in the sky. A security team can be very costly—just ask Britney Spears. It costs a lot of money to be left alone and feel safe.

During recent times, it has become increasingly more difficult to travel with luggage, which is unfortunate, because most of us prefer not to travel with a "come as you are" dress for all of our excursions. The airlines are now requiring a twenty-five dollar surcharge to check one bag. Is this fee to help pay for more rolls of duct tape?

Since most of us have decided to carry our luggage on the plane, each bag is x-rayed and inspected for weapon control. This means that any liquid containers that are over three ounces are confiscated as a possible act of terror. I just don't understand these new security rules at all. Did the military secretly interrogate a terrorist and gather this intelligence? "What size toiletries do you travel with? You will not leave this room until you tell us! I will ask you again and again … What size toi—"

"Okay … okay … I can't take it anymore! I prefer to travel with the larger bottles of toiletries. They must be over three ounces! Those little travel-size bottles really annoy me. I always run out!"

Because of this top secret information, my three-ounce shampoo bottle is really shampoo, but traveling with a four-ounce bottle of shampoo makes me a potential terrorist.

There was a story in the news recently about Paris Hilton being refused entry on the airplane after she showed up with a goat, a monkey, and a ferret. How does this happen? Paris shows up at the airplane with a petting zoo, and I get stopped if I have an eyelash curler in my bag!

Evidently, she was on a trip in Vegas, and won some money gambling and decided to buy some new pets while she was there. She was traveling back to L.A. and thought, why not take the entire family? They need a ride home, too!

After she was refused entry onto the plane, she took a six-hour limo ride back to L.A. I have taken limo rides before, too. It's a great way to travel! I've seen those big buses transporting horses while I'm driving on the highway. I don't know why they just don't put the poor horse in a limo! I guess some people aren't as concerned about their animals' comfort as Paris.

I know for a fact that the day Paris Hilton gets married, she will be registered at Petsmart! She already has jewelry, dishes, and linens; she needs dog food–lots of dog food–and whatever it is a goat eats!

Why is traveling so darn difficult anyhow?

Well, if you ask me, they have ALL gone completely "nuts."

3

Bless You

Isn't it amazing the stuff people will say to each other even though they have absolutely no idea what they are saying? I often remind my children that if you don't know what something means—DON'T SAY IT! But adults are guilty of breaking this violation all the time. How many times have you heard someone say "God Bless You!" after you sneeze? No one ever knows why they say this! They have either overheard someone else say it or when they sneezed, someone yelled "Bless You" for short.

There are many myths for saying "God Bless You" after someone sneezes. One theory is that during the Middle Ages when someone sneezed it was believed that an evil spirit left the body, so "Bless You" was said to protect the sneezer from harm. This is utterly ridiculous. The only evil spirit that is being expelled is SNOT! We are the ones who need to be protected from harm, not the sneezer! We are the victims from the Evil SNOT!

Why are we blessing the people who spread boogers on us? Why are they not blessing us? Even an apology would be appropriate. How about, "I'm sorry for sneezing in your face. Would you like me to pick the boogers out of your hair?"

When someone sneezes, their snot can travel at speeds of over 100 mph. We don't even have time to duck. We can't even protect ourselves and our loved ones. Why are we not given a warning as a courtesy?

If I am on the golf course and a ball is coming toward me, I am given a warning. The golfer yells "FORE" as loudly as he can as a courtesy so I have time to find cover to protect myself from the high velocity golf ball coming my way. If you know you are going to sneeze, you should be required to give a high velocity snot warning so that we have time to prepare. If you feel a sneeze comin' on, yell "TWO" as a warning so we can have time to move and cover our food.

I, myself, feel a little uncomfortable when someone says "God Bless You" when I sneeze. I usually sneeze in pairs and triplets, and rarely perform the single sneeze. I feel as though I should suppress the next wave of sneezes so that I don't inconvenience my well wisher with multiple "Bless Yous."

Have you ever noticed that the person who says "Bless You" usually stops after the first or second sneeze? It's because they are starting to feel like a complete idiot screaming "Bless You" and they don't even know why they are saying it!

The only thing more absurd is yelling "GESUNDHEIT" (pronounced guh-zoo nt-hahyt) after a sneeze.

Is this the stupidest sounding word? It is actually in the dictionary. Try and say "Gesundheit" three times in a row and tell me you don't feel like a complete idiot!

This is a word of German origin that people say when they hear someone sneeze. It means a wish of good health. Good Health! The sneezer is fine! We're the ones who are wondering if we are going to get sick the next day from breathing in wet, microscopic, yucky nose goop.

Why is no one concerned about us—the non-sneezers? Where is my support group? Why has no one started a support group for the victims of the sneezers!? No one cares about us!

Most people use either one word or the other. You never hear someone say "Bless You, Gesundheit, Bless You" for multiple sneezes. They pick the one they are most comfortable saying and stick with it.

There are three groups of people in the world: those who say "Bless You," those who say "Gesundheit," and those who are grossed out and reach for the hand sanitizer.

Guess which one I'm in?

Why are we so concerned with what we say to people when they sneeze? *Many of these people would not even stop to help if you were bleeding in the middle of the road,* but they seem to be the first to yell "God Bless You" for a snot blaster comin' their way.

There needs to be a standard protocol to follow for sneezing with an appropriate reply from the bystander:

First Sneeze	GROSS!!!
Second Sneeze	Watch out for my food!
Third Sneeze	Enough Already!
Fourth Sneeze	Go Home–You're Sick!

After the fourth sneeze, it should be assumed that the person is contagious with some type of cold or flu virus. At this time, you should think about saving yourself. This is a boogie war! Duck if you have to! Protect yourself and your loved ones from the spray of yucky, wet mucous mist.

There is an atheist father in California who filed a lawsuit to ban reciting the Pledge of Allegiance in a public classroom because he felt it was unconstitutional.

Saying the phrase "under God" in the Pledge of Allegiance made it all the way to the Supreme Court.

Does saying "God Bless You" in school when someone sneezes violate the separation of church and state as well?

What if an atheist sneezes and the kids have not yet learned the new standard protocol and bless him by mistake? If the kids don't yell "gross," the parents could file a lawsuit.

Is buying school lunches using coins and bills which state "In God We Trust" also a breach of the first amendment which separates religion and government?

What if my kid says "Thank God" or "Oh My God!" while they are at school—is this still legal? Why hasn't the school sent me an updated memo? I don't even know the rules!

"Uh ohhhh, y'all !!! I feel a really big sneeze comin' on … TWO … TWO … Achoooooooooooo! Ooooops … sorry! I think there is something in your hair!"

"GROSS!!! Melissa! Didn't anyone ever tell you it SNOT very nice to sneeze on your friends?"

Doesn't it seem a little ironic that the US Supreme Court opens each session with the invocation: "God save the United States and this Honorable Court"?

4

Traffic Law

Traffic signs are so confusing; they are really open to interpretation, that is the interpretation of each individual driver. The majority of us have not studied the driver's handbook since we took a driver's training course when we were sixteen years old. For many of the drivers on the road, that is a long, long time ago.

Just think, the majority of the drivers in Florida may have taken this course sixty to seventy years ago when they passed their written test. Did they even have the same street signs back then as they do now? Even the traffic signs they had twenty to thirty years ago may now be obsolete.

How are we supposed to remember what we learned thirty years ago when a majority of the population could not even recall what they ate for breakfast on a given day! I cannot even remember where I placed my car keys after each drive, but I am expected to retain all knowledge of the rules of the road from my driver's handbook from when I was in high school. New traffic signs keep poppin' up all over the place that I don't remember seeing before. There are no words; they are written with universal symbols.

The signs look like they were created by a kid in a kindergarten class who had progressed from drawing *stick people* to a new assignment of geometric shapes. This kiddie curriculum is now part of the No Kid Left Behind program initiated under the President Bush administration. This kindergarten geometry now defines our traffic laws.

The other drivers don't remember how to drive either. It's like a big guessing game out there on the road! Most people could not tell you what they are supposed to do at a flashing yellow light. Some drivers slow down, while others just come to a complete stop.

Have you ever seen drivers at a four-way stop? No one knows when it is their turn to go! They just kind of ease on out into the intersection a couple of feet at a time to make sure no one hits them.

One of the most annoying things that I have seen is when an emergency vehicle is coming toward you, but on the opposite side of the road and no one seems to know what the proper protocol is. Some cars will still pull over to the right side onto the shoulder of the road in case the ambulance or fire truck should need more room to pass; other cars just keep on going, oblivious to the shrieking sirens.

I admit that I don't know what the proper protocol is in all of these instances either. When a police officer pulls me over for a violation, the first thing they always ask is, "Do you know why I pulled you over?"

"I have no idea, officer. Why did you pull me over?" seems to be my standard reply. I am not playing stupid. I really don't know!

"Y'know, you made a U-turn in the middle of the intersection. That's why I pulled you over!"

"You mean that's not allowed!" I reply, completely baffled by this knowledge. "There was no sign that said 'No U-turn' there, so it was legal ... right?"

Where is the refresher course?

When kids study for the SATs for college admission, there is a review course. When lawyers and doctors take their state board exams, there is a refresher course. Most business professionals in the work place are continually taking courses of study related to their jobs. This is a requirement to keep up with the current changes in the workplace as it relates to a constantly changing and dynamic society. Even my hairdresser continually takes classes to learn the latest haircutting and style techniques! After we pass our driver's test and written test, we are set for life!

It does not matter that we do not remember anything we learned relating to the traffic signs. If you ask ten different people what a yield sign means, you may get ten different answers.

To yield, as defined by most current drivers, means to accelerate. It's a sign to put the pedal to the metal before the car in the main traffic lane catches up to you. It's a sign for: I'm gettin' ready to merge—watch out!

A yellow light is really just a soft green. You can still go, but you better go faster before the change to red. The real problem is when the car in front of you has a different interpretation of the soft green and decides to stop. You accelerate—he stops—not a good situation. This is the biggest reason for wear and tear on the brake pads!

As we age, our vision goes, our hearing goes, our reflexes go, our memory goes, but it does not matter! We took the driver's test at sixteen years old during our peak performance and cognitive ability.

We drivers on the road are part of an elite We Passed Club. Yep! We are the winners, not the failures. We are now road warriors who made it through this teenage rite of passage to the next phase of our life as kings and queens of the road.

For the remainder of our lives, we never need to learn another road sign again or even remember the ones we learned to pass the test.

One Test Per Person Per Lifetime.

That's The Traffic Law!

5

Stupid Questions?

People always say that there are no stupid questions. The only stupid questions are the ones you don't ask. I disagree. I think there are stupid questions, and there are stupid people. I also think there are smart people who ask stupid questions, and I think there are questions that should just not be asked.

I know this is true, because in my life I have heard many stupid questions. These questions are so stupid that if they were ever stated in a court of law and a jury had to decide the verdict of stupid or not stupid—that is the question— the jury would declare *stupid* in every case.

For instance, I have heard many stupid questions when I was a sales manager at a pharmaceutical company. I heard stupid questions in every venue, but this just seems to stand out most in my mind.

Oftentimes, these questions are asked during field visits when I am working with the sales reps while they are visiting with customers in their respective territories. During the car drives (sometimes long) from one office to another, we often chat about our family, houses, friends, and what the kids have been doing. Basically, we're just making chitchat to keep from sitting in awkward silence.

Since I spent so much time with the reps on a one-on-one basis, I made sure that when I hired them they passed the delightfulness test. This is actually a category that I decided to add to my interviews: a delightfulness category.

While the potential candidate is looking at me thinking, *I wonder what question she is going to ask me next*, I am looking at them thinking, *Could I sit in a closed car with this person for eight hours?* If the answer was no, it did not matter how qualified they were, how much experience they had, how many degrees they had—they were not going to be hired by me if they rate as a NO for delightfulness.

One of the worst situations would be to work with a rep in a closed car traveling at sixty miles an hour with no way out of that prison on wheels without doing a jump and roll.

I will share with you some, in my opinion, stupid questions.

I was traveling to a sales meeting and there were many sales reps on my flight. We were at the baggage claim awaiting the arrival of our luggage when one of the sales reps said, "I wonder when the plane with our luggage is going to arrive?"

Heeellllooo! Were we not all on the same plane? Is there a little plane that is carrying our luggage that is following the big plane?

I was working with one of my reps, who was building a house at the time. The rep could not decide between two different floor plans. "On one floor plan I like the upstairs, and on the other floor plan I like the downstairs. Can I just have the builder build the upstairs of one floor plan over the downstairs of the other floor plan?"

I had another rep who was also moving and building a house, and could not decide if they should pay the additional money to build a basement. So, he asked the question, "Couldn't we just decide if we want to add on the basement after we've lived in the house awhile?"

Now, c'mon, this is not like adding a sunroom on the main floor. I wanted to reply, "Yeah ... sure they can ... all they have to do is dig through the kitchen floor!"

I didn't say anything—sometimes silence is golden.

While working in my office one day, I received a phone call from a rep who became disheartened that her sales had gone down dramatically. She stated to me, "I just can't figure out why my sales are down. Do you think it would help if I start working on Mondays and Fridays again?"

I had a sales rep place a frantic phone call to me. She said that she needed to ask me a very urgent question. She had just gotten off the phone with one of her physicians and heard some terrible and disturbing news. The doctor had stated to her that one of his patients who had been taking our drug had just recently died.

After telling me the story of the patient, she asked me, "If a patient dies while taking our drug, would that be considered an adverse event? Should I report it?" Now, I think in this situation anyone with a little common sense could come to the right conclusion.

I realize this is just my opinion, but c'mon, these are stupid questions!

What amazes me is that if you are in a group setting and someone in front of the group asks a question, and even goes on to preface it with, "I know this is a stupid question, but I'm going to ask it anyway," the reply is always the same.

"No, Tyler, there are no stupid questions. The only stupid questions are the ones you don't ask."

So then, given this encouragement, Tyler goes ahead and asks his stupid question. And, of course, it is as stupid as they always are when someone starts off with, "This maybe a stupid question but. . . . "

And, of course, the presenter answers the question with a straight face while thinking to himself, *I can't wait to share this one with my colleagues when we meet up for drinks at the bar*!

Then, to make matters worse, after the question is answered with a straight face, without a hint of sarcasm, the next comment from the presenter is always, "Thank you, Tyler, for asking that question. I'm sure there were a lot of other people in the group who had the same question, but were afraid to ask."

Tyler is now a HERO as he is lauded for his bravery in asking this question. Bravery is no longer defined as fighting on the front line of the battlefield; it is now defined as having the courage to ask a completely ridiculous question in front of a group.

What's up with this? Is this stupid question etiquette!? Did someone hear someone else say these comments from a prestigious speaker presenting at a seminar when a person asked a stupid question and this was how it was handled?

How did this become the golden rule of etiquette for stupid questions?

6

Matzo Ball Soup

I was at the dentist's office talking to the dental technician and saying that I was preparing for my son's Bar Mitzvah. She replied, "Oh, you're Jewish? I didn't know you were Jewish!" (I'm thinking, *I must have run out of the house without my Star of David. I forgot to tattoo it on my forehead today.*)

Then she said, "How long have you been Jewish?"

I said, "Since birth . . . I was born that way."

She looked at me like it was a birth defect. Since birth? You've had this condition since birth? Is it treatable?

It's as if she thought it was a decision you made when you got out of bed in the morning. Let's see, should I be Jewish today or should I be a vegetarian? I can't decide!!! I think I'll be Jewish until noon, then I'll be a vegetarian in the afternoon!

There are very few Jewish people in the area of Atlanta where we live. Usually, when I mention that I am Jewish, the first thing people say to me is, "There's a guy by the name of Mintz who is a Jew in Louisiana. Do you know him?" or "I knew a Jewish person in Texas once. I forgot their name—you must know that family."

"I knew a Mintz once when I was a kid. That's your cousin . . . right?"

Why do people think we all know each other???

Do they think there is some Jewish Network where we all get together once a year for a weekend at a nice resort, just hang out and party, and do a meet and greet?

"Ohhhhh yeahhhhhh, I've heard of you. You're that Jew in Texas someone was asking me about."

"Oh, hi!!! So glad to finally meet you. I heard there was a Mintz somewhere else in the country! I am glad we could finally meet!!!"

Just last week I was in a sewing store with Morgan to pick up the damaged sewing machine that Brandon dropped on the living room tile floor. "What's your last name, and I'll check if it's finished?" the sales lady said as she looked for our name tag on all the repaired sewing machines in the storage room.

"It's Mintz," I said. " . . . M-I-N-T-Z."

As soon as I said the Z, she was running toward me from the storage room. "You must know my friends in Raleigh—the Mintz's. You're related, RIGHT???? Are you Jewish? They're our only Jewish friends."

"Of course I do!" I replied. "I have photos of them in my purse in the car. I'll bring them in next time!"

I could see how excited she was with the confirmation that yes indeed, we *are* all related, so I continued, "We usually travel to Raleigh to see them for their annual Fourth of July kosher chicken barbecue with potato knishes and her special matzo green bean casserole. It's absolutely delicious!!! Mintz family recipe, y'know."

I have always thought it was strange when I hear a conversation and it starts off like this: "Me and my Jewish friend Howie went out last night to a baseball game and watched the Braves beat the Astros 7-3. My Jewish friend and I had six beers between us and threw peanuts at the idiot a few rows in front of us who started cheering for the Astros.

"'Go back to Houston with your humidity and flat topography!'" my Jewish friend Howie yelled.

"It was hilarious. Those Jews, so funny and full of nonsense! They all are! The Jew Howie even paid for my beers. What a nice Jewish boy . . . that Howie!"

I have never heard a conversation in my life that starts off with, "I went bar hopping last night with some friends from work: my black friend Tamika and my Catholic friend Mary. We danced aaaaallllll night long. Mary brought her Baptist boyfriend along. I think his name might have been John. I was a little tipsy, but I remember he was a Baptist!"

For some reason, that I have yet to figure out, many people use the qualifier Jewish either before or after your first name. My friend David, who's Jewish, or it could be said my Jewish friend

David. It's just a personal preference, I guess. Most people seem to have their favorite way of doing it and stick to it.

So . . . if you do know any other Melissas, as I am sure there must be a few more of us, I guess I am the Melissa, who's Jewish, or the Jewish friend Melissa. I am so confused!!! I don't know how to do it right!

By the way, for all of you who are wondering, I do not know Adam Sandler. We are not related! But, I heard from a Jew, who heard it from another Jew, who heard it from a Jewish girl at the Jewish Network that he was seen at a deli eating Matzo Ball Soup!

Thank goodness we all stay connected!

So, as it turns out, I am probably not related to any of you, so please don't drop by when you are in Atlanta. It's just me and my two "junior mintz."

The local grocery store has a little Jewish section with Matzo Ball soup mix, Matzo, and some other kosher foods. It's located near the other ethnic foods like the Taco Bell taco kit and salsa. Whenever I stand in front of this "little section," I always see nearby shoppers pause to look over there. "Oh look! There's someone in the Jewish section. I wonder if we have a Jew living here? Nope, she's probably from out of town."

Since there are very few Jewish families who live in this area, I always scrutinize the expiration dates on the food. *Let's see, how long has this box of Matzo been sitting on the shelf. I haven't bought Matzo in a long time. How many years has this box been sitting here?*

Most people know very little about Judaism. I remember when my son had his Bar Mitzvah, none of his friends had ever been to one. They had heard that this is the ceremony where he "becomes a man."

I have heard this many times as well, and I always think it sounds strange. My little thirteen-year-old boy. How is he a man? He is not even driving yet! Whenever I hear this, I always think of those Hollywood movies where they switch places … like the Walt Disney movie *Freaky Friday* with Lindsay Lohan and Jamie Lee Curtis.

In the movie, Lindsay is a teenager who switches places with her mom (Jamie Lee Curtis). Her mom then becomes a teenager and Lindsay is now the mom. They are trapped in each other's bodies until they find a way to switch back. It's like Brandon is standing on the bimah in the Temple and he switches places with the Rabbi and becomes a man. The Rabbi is now a thirteen-year-old boy. When the Bar Mitzvah ceremony is completed, they switch back and are in their own bodies again.

Our dear Rabbi Winokur never knew what hit him. Brandon had to repeatedly ask him to keep quiet and stop fidgeting during the ceremony!

Brandon went on to explain to his friends that he does not become a man, but in the Jewish tradition he is now responsible for his own actions. He is the one responsible for continuing with his Jewish education, not his parents. Brandon did a flawless job leading the congregation in prayer and reading from the Torah. We were all so proud! All of his friends had a great time at the dinner party hosted by my mom.

Rabbi Winokur is still trying to figure out his newfound passion for playing video games!

Since I am the local Jew Mom, my daughter's teacher asked me if I would come in to school one day to talk to the class about Hanukkah. She thought it would be a good idea if the kids were exposed to traditions from another religion.

I said, "Sure, I'll do it! I'll bring in a small book to read about Hanukkah and the war with the Maccabees. I'll even bring in some dreidels for the class to play with!"

When I showed up at the school for my fifteen-minute Hanukkah talk, I saw hundreds of kids lined up in the hallway. "Where are all of these kids going?" I asked in my usual barely audible rambling as my mind started to race. "Is there an assembly that is going to conflict with my Hanukkah talk to my daughter's class?" I continued, still talking to myself.

All of a sudden, the teacher came out into the hall and said, "Oh, by the way, I mentioned to some of the other teachers that there was going to be a Hanukkah talk and a dreidel demonstration. They decided that their students should be exposed to this talk as well."

So now my play with the dreidels has become a dreidel demonstration and my little talk is now a "school assembly." I was waiting for the announcement for the school assembly, "Jew Mom here for Hanukkah talk and dreidel demonstration. Please proceed quietly to the assembly."

I felt like an exhibit at the zoo. Here we have a Jewish Mother. She celebrates Hanukkah and has been trained to use a dreidel. She likes to eat potato latkes fried in oil.

I was herded to the assembly room and onto the stage with my little book about Hanukkah and my bag of dreidels. I stood up there with pride thinking of how my years of training as a pharmaceutical sales rep and sales manager have made me a seasoned professional at public speaking.

I was delighted that I felt no jitters at performing the #1 most dreaded task: public speaking. According to all the marketing polls that have been conducted for the most fearful event, #1 on the list is public speaking, and #2 on the list is dying.

Just think; *people would rather die than speak to elementary school kids about the miracle of Hanukkah!*

As I started the lecture with my *Complete Guide to Hanukkah* book that is so little it fits into the palm of my hand, I read about the miracle of Hanukkah and the lighting of the menorah. I discussed how Hanukkah is really a miracle about religious freedom.

"A tyrant king destroyed the Temple of the Jews because they refused to worship idols. In this destruction, the oil that was used to light the menorah was spilled," I explained, trying not to be too detailed and boring.

"The Jews won the war against the king; then they repaired and cleaned the temple. They lit the menorah to rededicate the temple, but there was only enough oil to last for one day," I continued with the story.

"Miraculously, the oil lasted for eight days. The menorah continued to be lit until more oil could be made. This is why we celebrate Hanukkah for eight days," I said to conclude the talk.

Then, I proceeded with my dreidel demonstration and explained the rules of play. The big hit, of course, was the chocolate money (Hanukkah gelt) we used to play the dreidel game. When the questions came, it was all about the chocolate money and the dreidel game.

Thank goodness I brought in some bags of chocolate money to give to my daughter's class to play dreidel. Instead of giving each kid in her class their own bag of coins as originally planned, I ripped those little nylon bags open and each kiddie got one chocolate coin.

I have learned from experience, when you speak to kids, you should bring in cookies or candy, or they will think you are the worst guest speaker ever! They may not remember what you said, but they will remember if the cookies were yummy!

I only brought in enough candy to last for *one* class, but miraculously the chocolate lasted for *eight* classes. This is a Hanukkah miracle!

7

Road Rage

As I was driving down the road with my daughter Morgan, she saw a car in front of us that had a personalized license plate. Morgan said, "Hey Mom, why don't you get a personalized license plate? That would be soooooo cooooool."

For a brief moment, I envisioned driving down the road with a cute personalized plate with a Hot Mom tag for all to see. As soon as the thought came, it vanished just as quickly. I realized something of great importance—I AM A BAD DRIVER!

I know this to be true. I have been told this by everyone who has driven with me, everyone who has seen me drive, and everyone who has just heard about my driving. Even in my company I am known as a really bad driver. No one wants to get in a car with me. I have had bosses who have worked with me and said, "Next time we work together, I'm driving. You can be the passenger!"

I consider myself to be an aggressive driver. Some people mistakenly refer to this as bad driving. They are just confused and don't know any better, I constantly remind myself. The truth is when I see an opportunity on the road, I take it. If I am trying to switch lanes and the car behind me is slowing down, I'll speed up to merge.

It's efficiency, really. It's because of me that the traffic in Atlanta is flowing as it should be during the day. I am not the slowpoke waiting for all the other drivers to practically come to a complete stop every time I want to get over a lane.

I feel that you really need to be a little more aggressive driving these days. Have you noticed that people seem to be more in a hurry than ever to get wherever they are going? I rarely meet any nice and courteous drivers on the road anymore.

Whenever I put my turn signal on to merge to the next lane, cars speed up. I may even be part of the way over into the next lane and a car will cut me off, then honk at me! It's as if they think they actually own the entire road in front of them and beyond—to infinity! *It's my lane and I did not give you permission to come over. Get to the back of the line!*

What's the deal with the honking as soon as the light turns green!? Is my eye and foot coordination not fast enough for some of you people? This is one of my biggest driving pet peeves.

This is what happens when people play too many video games: their brains are fried and scrambled like an egg. They are now conditioned to have an automatic reaction every time a new visual stimulus enters their small squishy brain.

Their perception of the world now becomes a giant video game screen. "There is a new color that entered my screen; a green light has just entered my brain field. React! React! React!"

Shouldn't there be at least a two-second rule before the horn blaring starts by the "burned-out brain" idiot behind me.

Y'know what I do? Nothing. I just sit there for a few more seconds to really piss them off. When most people hear the horn, their automatic reflexes take over, and they press on the gas. Not me. I count to three and, in between the numbers, I say, "Mississippi," real slowly.

I do finally go at my leisure with my parade wave, minus the thumb and three fingers. It's more like a single finger wave; it could even be called a gesture. But, I like to refer to it as my one-finger parade wave. After all, I live in the South and we try to remain civil. So I do the Southern thing; I smile while doing it just to be friendly.

I am a courteous driver. If I see that a car has a turn signal on, I slow down, not speed up. If there is a car trying to merge back into traffic from an off-road amenity such as a gas station or a store, I wave them in front of me and I always do the thank you hand wave on the rare occasion of courtesy from another driver.

Who made up the *thank you parade wave* when we drive? Who is in charge of making up these universal hand signals? I have a few hand signals that I would like to be put on the list, too.

I wouldn't really call it a wave. Maybe a double, single finger parade wave. "Hey, look y'all, I'm drivin' with no hands." If only I knew who to call!

I had one, what I now consider to be, really good driving day. The day I passed my driver's test! No one actually admits to being a bad driver, unless you, as the driver, are actually afraid of your own driving. Okay, I will admit, there are a few times that my driving could be a little too aggressive.

I am constantly changing lanes as a last-minute decision and I love the U-turn. I really do. I am a huge fan of making U-turns all day long. I constantly miss a turn because I am paying attention to off-road amenities like new restaurants that have opened up, people walking their cute little doggies, and a beautiful flowery tree that recently bloomed.

The road is boring. It's not very attractive, and there is just not much to look at. It's not my fault nobody cared about making the roads a little more scenic. Why do we have so much black and gray asphalt? You think by now another color would be in style; pink and yellow would be nice, blue and green, maybe some orange, too—just not boring and dreary gray.

When it's rainy and foggy we can't even see the road because it's so ugly! It just blends into the atmosphere or something.

I wonder what the allotted daily allowance for U-turns might be. Is this what they would teach us if we had a mandatory driver review course? How many U-turns each person is allotted per day? If other family members don't use all of theirs, can we use them? Are they transferable?

These are the things we should all know. This is the problem with drivers today; nobody knows the answers to any of these questions. Some days it's like I get behind the wheel of a car, and I turn into a completely different person. As soon as I sit behind the wheel of my own personalized tank, I have no fear. I will rule the road with this piece of "steel on wheels." I am invincible! I am woman!

I actually make my own self carsick!

I have thought about taking those little barf bags from the airplane and placing them in the glove box of my car just to be a good car hostess in case a passenger is not feeling well. I usually keep gum and candy in the car to offer my guests. Why not a barf bag? Besides, the airlines waste so much money making all of these little white bags and no one ever takes them.

I might as well put them to good use. After all, I already paid for it; it came with my seat. Just like the cost of my ticket paid for my bag of peanuts and one small beverage of my choice. One bag per seat! I am tired of wasting money. I'm takin' my bag and the one for the guy whose butt is crammed next to mine on my next flight. *I paid enough for my seat. All this is mine ... mine ... mine!*

So ... as I was sayin' .... .

People who drive like me don't get personalized license plates—we like our anonymity!

I don't want the person who is behind me in traffic when I cut in front of them to say, "That's Melissa again with her Hot

Mom plate." I like that when I do a boo-boo on the road, no one knows who is driving the mystery car.

Bad drivers don't get personalized license plates. We get tinted windows! We need to protect our identity.

What could be more fun than driving down the road with tinted windows! If I am not happy with the other drivers on the road, I can stick out my tongue, make weird faces, do my one-finger parade wave, all with complete privacy.

I have heard people say that Las Vegas is like Disneyland for adults. Vegas isn't Disneyland—driving in your car with tinted windows is much more of an amusement.

I lucked out and had one good day and got a driver's license. It's been a steady decline ever since that one fortunate day!

Do tinted windows just encourage people to pick their nose more? What's up with this behavior? I drive all day long making sales calls and I look to my right and look to my left, and I see this every day. What is going on? Do people pick their nose to the beat of their favorite song? "Good beat … love that song. I'm bored, not too much traffic today. I'll pick my nose on two and four, right on the beat! I'll grab one from my left nostril on two and one from my right nostril on four just so I don't run out."

All of a sudden people put their car in drive and a finger goes up their nostril! Is this behavior somehow encoded in our DNA? When we get in a car, we pick our nose? Do our ancestors, the apes, pick their noses, too? For that matter, every time I have been to the zoo, I have never seen an animal pick their nose. I have never even seen my dog pick its nose.

I remember in elementary school we learned that what differentiates us from our primate ancestors is the fact that we humans have a working thumb. Yes, we actually use our thumb, and this, apparently, is a very important differentiation. Because of our "working thumb" feature, we are primates that stand erect and enjoy shopping, driving cars, and working for a living.

There are actually two features that differentiate us from our so-called ape ancestors. Humans can use their thumb and can put a finger up their nostril.

Why have our science books never been updated with this new breakthrough discovery? This is a newsworthy (or nose-worthy) discovery.

Why has CNN never been alerted? This news should be on 24 hours a day! This defines who we are! Doesn't anyone even care about the humans?!

Without this unique feature we could be an endangered species!

Did you ever see a whale pick its nose? Of course not, and now they are endangered!!!

SAVE THE HUMANS! Where are all the posters?

Many people have stopped smoking, but we still seem to have ashtrays in our cars. More people pick their nose in their cars than smoke. Should we start calling the ashtrays—booger trays!?

When people buy a car, the salesperson says, "And this is your ashtray," while doing their overview of the car features. Our first thought is always, *Why are car manufacturers still putting ashtrays in our cars? The people who smoke never use them. They don't want to dirty the ashtray in their own cars.*

They roll down the window! I have never seen anyone who smokes use an ashtray. For that matter, I have never seen a dirty cigarette-filled ashtray in any car I have ever been in! But, I have seen hundreds of drivers roll down their windows to toss ashes and cigarette butts. These smokers have made the entire planet their own personal ashtray!

If Walter, the salesperson, says when pointing to the tray formerly known as the ashtray, "This is your booger tray," people would say, "Oh yeah, great idea. I always wondered what I should do with those little boogers!"

I decided to go to the car dealership to see my friend, Walter. I wanted to find out how the new cars are selling with the updated trays. I see Walter pulling into the dealership lot with a teenager driving a bright blue metallic Camaro.

"Hi, Walter," I yelled and waved.

"Oh . . . hello," he politely said. "This is Danny. He's thinking of buying this car."

"Hey, Walt," Danny said, after he finished his test drive in the new Camaro he was considering buying. "I want to show you why I think the booger tray in the new cars are such a great selling feature," Danny said as he was looking behind him to make sure Walt was following closely as he was walking to his car.

"Look at my car! These are the fresh ones that I picked while listening to Metallica's 'Fade to Black.' Had to flick 'em on the dash in front of the passenger seat! I never knew where to flick 'em before, Walter. Now I know the perfect place to put them in my new Camaro! And if I should need them later (snack), I know just where they'll be!"

Have you ever thought that shaking hands with people is really an obsolete greeting?

Maybe we should just wave. I don't know where your hands have been??!

8

Pretty Toilet

One of my favorite vacations to go with the kids is the beach. We try to plan a beach vacation every year during the kids' summer break. I love going to the beach and swimming in the ocean. There is such a feeling of calmness and serenity to hear the sounds of the ocean waves as they come crashing toward the shoreline and topple over to create a beautiful white frothy cap that seems to lull us into a sense of peacefulness.

The feel of the cool summer breeze blowing softly against our bodies helps to balance the direct heat from the sun on a cloudless and beautiful, sunny summer day. Immense colors of the water that range from an emerald green to a turquoise blue seem to fill our hearts with beauty and wonderment.

The soft warm sand beneath our feet and between our toes creates a warmth that travels through our entire bodies as we walk along the shorelines.

Seeing the vastness of the water reminds us of how small we really are compared to the seemingly borderless expanse of the ocean.

Swimming in the ocean is an *experience of the senses of creation,* as we feel the strength of the ocean's current while we are bathed in the jewel-colored waters.

With all of this profound beauty it is difficult to believe that we are swimming in the little fishies' toilet! When I take my kids to the beach and they ask me if they can pee in the ocean, I just tell them, "The little fishies do it!"

Yep, this is where it all happens. The fish and the rest of the aquatic life live here, eat here, sleep here, and go to the bathroom here. They never have to flush the toilet! Have you ever seen a fish argue about who left the toilet seat up? Of course not; they are swimming in the largest toilet bowl in the world.

My children love to travel to the beach. When we are deciding how and where to spend our summer vacation, there is always a trip to the beach planned because my kids love swimming in the toilet, and so do I!

It is my favorite place to go. I love all the beautiful colors of the toilet bowl. I love feeling the waves and the heat of the sun's rays bathe me in warmth. I love the fact that the sea animals allow us in their bathroom and don't care if we are in there playing and swimming as they are doing "their business."

Some of nature's toilet bowls are prettier than others. I especially like my toilet water a nice turquoise blue when I swim. I also like the water to be clear so I can see what's going on beneath the surface. If I am walking into the ocean and I feel something squishy beneath my feet, I want to see if it's seaweed or if I am standing on a sea creature and hurting his little back. If there is a big fish or a shark coming to greet me, I want to be able to see him coming and greet him appropriately. If there is something nibbling at my toes, I want to see what it is. Is this too much to ask for?

I want a clean toilet bowl!! Our aquatic friends are not able to flush their toilets like we are. When their home becomes polluted, they live in filth every day.

On our last vacation I decided to take the kids snorkeling. I thought it would be a good idea to swim with some of the native fish. As I was swimming around by the reef, I saw a cute little, brightly-colored orange fish. From a distance it looked like a clownfish and I wanted to follow him to get a closer look.

As I approached from behind, I decided to introduce myself so I wouldn't startle him. "Heeellllooo! . . . Melissa here, on vaca . . . you may not recognize me with my new mask!" He turned around and swam over to greet me. The little orange clownfish fish seemed to be swimming around me a lot slower than all the other fish feeding on the reef.

I thought this fish looked really familiar, but I couldn't remember where I had seen him before. When I finally caught up to the slow–moving clownfish, I could not believe who it was. "Oh my gosh! Oh my gosh!" I excitedly repeated into my now water-filled snorkel.

A familiar face in this great expanse of the ocean. I could not believe my luck. With 73 trillion fish in the ocean I ran into a celebrity. A big-time movie star!

I got right up to him and called out to get his attention. "Nemo! Nemo!" I yelled. "I was wondering if I could get a picture with you for my kids. They'll never believe I met such a famous movie star."

Nemo looked up at me and started to talk, but before any words came out he was gasping to catch his breath. "All drains lead into the ocean," he said, still trying to catch his breath. "My wise old friend, Gill, once told me that."

"What?" I said softly, not sure what this had to do with my big photo opportunity.

"Gill was right, y'know," he continued, then paused and placed an inhaler in his little mouth and took two puffs.

"Are you okay?" I asked Nemo, very concerned about his health. I started to study him and noticed he didn't look well at all. He was definitely quite a bit older now, his skin sickly and pale. Nemo was much thinner than when he was on the big screen. He was huffing and puffing. When he spoke he had to constantly stop to catch his breath.

Nemo shifted his eyes downward toward the ocean floor before speaking again. "I have asthma now," he said in the most heartrending voice. "Many of the other fish are sick now, too." He continued talking while still averting his eyes from me. "We are sick with the same conditions you humans suffer from."

"Nemo, I don't understand any of this!" I stammered. "How could something like this have happened?"

Nemo seemed to look shocked and surprised that I didn't know how this could have happened. He was talking a little faster now. "The humans knew what they were doing, but they didn't seem to care." He then continued on and on, talking when he could and resting when he needed a break. His voice was weak and would lose strength as he explained what had happened to his life.

"When I was a little kid still in fishergarten, I didn't understand why my dad was so concerned with us living by a reef in pristine water. He would say to me, 'Nemo, take a deep breath and soak in this beautiful view! The water is so clear I can see for miles. Ahhhh . . . so easy to breathe here!'

"After a short time, everything started to change." He paused briefly and took another puff from his inhaler. "The water started to get cloudy and our visibility was poor. The fish couldn't even see where to lay their eggs. The baby fish started to die as their parents became ill and couldn't care for them. Every day it was becoming more and more difficult to breathe.

"My dad and I even went to our usual vacation spot at the Clear Water Resort. It's a nice fish hotel near Florida. It was such a beautiful place. The water was always so clear, and the coral was bright and beautiful. The plant life was lush with varying shades of vibrant green. We always had so much fun there. We would ride the fishie wheel at the amusement park during the day. At night my dad and I would go to our favorite restaurant Shark Bait and eat freshly prepared raw shrimp."

"How is your dad?" I asked cautiously, not knowing what to expect.

"He's not doing well at all. His health is rapidly deteriorating. Lately, he's been in and out of the Blue Gill Medical Center. He has a problem with his gills and is not taking in enough oxygen. He has been straining to breathe for so long that his gills have started to collapse."

Nemo continued where he left off before I interjected. He seemed really glad to have someone to just . . . listen.

"My dad would often say, 'Nemo, you should really cherish these times.' I never really knew what he meant, but now I know. He meant that there are fewer and fewer places that aren't polluted."

He went on and on talking about the illnesses of his friends and family. He explained how Dory first ended up with short-term memory problems due to the mercury in the water. "Dory now has long-term memory problems. Sometimes she can't remember anything for days. She just swims around in a circle because she doesn't remember where she wants to go. She rarely says hello anymore. She doesn't even remember me most of the time."

Nemo explained how the storm drains cause a lot of the pollution. "Your trash is our trash," he said, still trying to educate me. "Why is your garbage littered all over the place?" He waited for a response from me, but I didn't have one.

He talked about all the lead that was being dumped daily into the water from batteries that weren't being disposed of properly. "Lead doesn't go away," he said. "The lead from your paint and batteries ends up in soil, carried to the nearest water supply, and eventually ends up in my front yard. I have several cousins," he paused to catch his breath, "and an uncle who were poisoned and sank to the bottom of the ocean."

"I'm so sorry," I said.

I wasn't even aware that car exhaust emissions and the oil from an oil change ended up in the ocean too, but Nemo taught me how. "An average oil change from one car can contaminate close to a million gallons of water," he said.

"I had no idea, Nemo," I replied.

He explained that when the oil is dumped on the ground it either goes into the soil or is carried by the rain down the sewer system and storm drains to the nearest body of water.

"Nemo, what about the car emissions?" I asked. "How does this get into the water?"

"What goes up must come down," he said. "This pollution falls to the ground, gets carried by the rain, and ends up at my house, too."

"What do you do for a living?" he asked.

"I'm a drug rep and a writer," I responded. I was surprised to hear him chuckle at this.

"That's pretty cool," he said. "It just sounds perfect! Could you do me a favor?" Nemo asked.

"Sure . . . anything," I said.

"Could you help me refill my prescription and also write about what is happening in the ocean? Who knows—maybe people can change. Maybe one day I'll have a family and they will be able to enjoy a clean home."

"I promise, Nemo. I will help you and write your book. I'll be your voice," I told him. And I meant it.

As I turned to swim away, I heard Nemo's faint little voice: "I really like your new mask."

The ocean water made it impossible to feel the tears that started streaming down my cheek, but I knew they were there. My eyes continued to tear and burn with anger. I started to hate the humans for what they did to Nemo. I hated them for what they did to his friends and family. Then I realized—I was one of them.

As I digested this knowledge, my stomach felt queasy. I thought I was going to be sick. I wanted to help Nemo and his fish family. *Just as soon as I get home I will write this book and tell his story*, I vowed to myself. I was more determined than ever to find a way to let people know how much our sea friends are suffering.

"Kiiiiddddssss!" I yelled to Morgan and Brandon, who were chasing a school of brightly-colored fish on the other side of the reef. "It's time to go home—our vacation is over! Your mom is writing a book for a famous movie star. He just hired me to be his ghost writer."

As soon as I got home, I started on Nemo's book. I wrote whenever I could find some time. I would make notes in my daytimer as I was waiting for the doctor. I wrote early in the morning before I needed to get ready for work. After the kids went to bed, I would stay up for several hours and continue to write.

"Why are you doing this?" my kids would ask me. "It just seems like a lot of work for nothing!" Brandon would say whenever he saw me write.

"Because ... I'm helping a friend, and he's helping his friends. Sometimes we all need to work together. If you met someone who needed help and you thought you could, wouldn't you at least try?"

"I guess I would," they both said, but I knew they still didn't get it.

"Okay ... it's like this ... you know how when we go someplace and the only toilets are those porta-potties that you can't flush? All the waste just piles up in one place. Well ... right now that's where Nemo lives. Could you live there?"

"That's disgusting, Mom!" they both yelled. "Help him get out of there!!!" *I'm glad we finally agree on something*, I thought and decided not to gloat.

After several months, I finally finished Nemo's memoir. I wanted to share Nemo's story with the world and make his book available to kids everywhere. Nemo had hoped that all parents would read his story to their children so that they can grow up to be more aware of their actions and take better care of the planet, where this could never happen again.

I promised Nemo that I would travel around the country and talk to school kids about the hazards of ocean pollution on the little fishies, as well as on the plants and animals. After traveling all over the country on a book and lecture tour, I had only one school left. It was my daughter's school, so I wanted to save it for last.

I started the talk just as I have done at least a hundred times before, but this time it felt different. I felt like people were starting to listen now and the buzz about the book was spreading around the globe. People were saddened when they initially heard about Nemo. He was their friend. Nemo was someone they knew and loved. They really did want to help; they just weren't sure how.

I took the stage and started my talk the way I have always done. "This book is based on a true story. The title is *Why Nemo Couldn't Breathe.*

"Once upon a time, the people of planet Earth enjoyed clean air and clean water. The water was pristine and clear, and the fish and sea animals were happy and healthy. Fish was a big part of their diet. The kids enjoyed crispy oven-baked fish sticks for lunch, usually with tartar sauce or ketchup."

As I continued reading the first chapter, I talked about how everything gradually changed and the ocean became so polluted that many of the fish were now unsafe for us to eat. I was now at the end of chapter two and read the last sentence to the kids: "This is how the mercury entered through Dory's gills and affected her brain."

As I finished this chapter, the room became so silent you could hear a pin drop. Most of the kids had never even heard about mercury toxicity. They had no idea that their beloved Dory was suffering from mercury poisoning, which traveled to her brain and caused her memory loss.

In chapter two, I had read to them about how most of the mercury comes from the coal burning power plants. It was very important to Nemo that the kids understand how the mercury pollutes our air. His hope was that if children were educated, one day in the near future we would have better pollution control devices, and we'd all enjoy cleaner air. I read this part to the kids exactly as it was written.

"Mercury is naturally in the coal, and when the coal is burned to generate electricity, we can see the mercury emissions leaving the building by the black air coming from the smoke stacks. The mercury then pollutes the air and gets into the water when it rains."

When I finished, I heard a boy in the front row scream out, "They need to breathe in oxygen, too!"

"That's right!" I said, realizing they really were paying attention and seemed to understand that we are suffocating our ocean friends. Since he was sitting in front of me, I asked him his name.

"It's Mark," he said shyly, wondering what he'd just gotten himself into.

"Well, Mark, what you said was true! Our ocean friends are breathing in polluted oxygen in the water just as we breathe in polluted oxygen in our air. *Polluted water and polluted air are the same thing—our life force being destroyed.*"

After I said this to the entire auditorium, I saw all of Mark's classmates turn to look at him. A few kids that were seated around him patted him on the back. Mark looked over at his teacher who was beaming with pride. *That's my student!* I knew she was thinking.

By the time I got to the last chapter, *Finding Nemo 2,* there was hardly a dry eye in the house. "Hollywood kept calling me to work on the sequel to *Finding Nemo,* but I was too sick; I couldn't work. I knew I really let my fans down. This is what I am most upset about."

I felt bad when a few of the kids started crying, so I decided to tell them a funny story that Nemo shared with me that day we met in the ocean.

"This is a story that Nemo shared with me the last time I saw him," I said, hoping to cheer them up a little bit. "Kids . . . this is how he started the story. . . .

"'Melissa, did I tell you the story of how Buzz Lightyear ended up at my front door? Whenever garbage is discarded on land, the rain washes it down the storm drains and it eventually ends up at my house. Remember, we have already talked about this,' Nemo said, and then he continued with his story. 'Just newly arrived today, I have a McDonald's cup in my front yard. All kinds of plastic soda and water bottles, six plastic army men, two cigarette lighters, and a Buzz Lightyear that says, 'To infinity and beyond!' when you pull the string.'

"'How did you get a Buzz Lightyear?' I had asked him.

"'Who knows,' Nemo said. 'It could have been left at the beach or thrown off a boat. But underwater, Buzz sounds like he is saying, 'Two fins and beans!' a popular delicacy in my home town. 'Two fins, and beans!' Nemo said again as he laughed, coughed, then took two puffs from his inhaler.

"'I actually met Buzz at the premier of *Finding Nemo*. He showed up with Woody. I was sitting in a small fish tank with Gill and Dory in the third row end seat on the left aisle. Buzz and Woody just plopped down in the two open seats next to us.' Nemo stopped for a moment to catch his breath, then continued. 'Great guys really, but during the premiere Buzz kept yelling, 'To infinity and beyond!' at the most inappropriate times. It was funny at first, but I was a little embarrassed by him actually. 'I'm the only sheriff in town!' Woody yelled as he whipped his gun from the holster and pointed it at Buzz. 'This movie theater is not big enough for the both of us!' At first, Dory was really scared and sandwiched herself between me and Gill, who was laughing hysterically at the whole scene. Finally, a defeated Buzz slumped down into his seat, and we all got to watch the rest of the movie in peace.'

"Well kids," I said with a sighed relief that I still remembered the conversation, "that's the end of the story. See ... Nemo still has his sense of humor!"

I looked around the auditorium one last time and noticed the kids were smiling now and many of them were still laughing about the story. Two boys toward the back of the room were acting out the Woody scene. They were pretending to pull out imaginary guns from the holster to see who had the fastest draw.

I ended the book with the statement that Nemo had asked me to write. He said he wanted to leave the humans with a very simple message:

"Let's all help the little fishies clean their toilets. It's really nice of them to let us swim."

"Nemo . . . this is for you, little buddy!" I said softly to myself as I left the stage for the last time. "This is for you."

9

Evolution

When I was in school we were taught during our science class that human beings evolved from apes. They showed us a chart which displayed the progression from ape to man during the different stages of evolution. In each picture, we are gradually standing more upright as we continue the journey of time to human.

Who made this stuff up? Who said that way back in my family tree I have apes for relatives? For the record, I am not denying the possibility of my relatives being from the primate family. There have been times when I have looked at a few of them and thought, *What a striking resemblance!*

I even have one relative in particular who has a close resemblance to an orangutan that I saw at the zoo. Not just because of the facial expressions, but her mannerisms as well.

Sometimes the way she would laugh reminded me of how orangutans smiled with their mouth wide open and all their teeth showing. She also had the short, reddish-brown hair that is the standard hairstyle of this primate.

All of the orangutans must have the same hairstylist and colorist. HELLO! Maybe it's time for a change. If you see all of your ape friends with the same hairstyle, it may be time to go blond!

I have even dated guys that I am sure are the first generation in their family to actually stand erect! You can easily spot a newbie who has just recently evolved. The newbies all have distinct characteristics.

Here's some examples to help you spot the newbie in your life:

The guys with excessive facial and body hair; the ones that have their wives or girlfriends shave their backs for swimsuit season.

The guy in your life who dislikes having to make conversation and answers most questions with a one syllable response—usually a yes or no, but is sometimes only a grunt.

Men who love contact sports and are overly competitive (survival of the fittest mentality). They like to wear little tank tops to show grossly-oversized muscles, are commitment phobic, and love camping out in the woods (with no tent and no bathrooms).

Another newbie behavior is eating too much fruit and nut mix from the grocery store!

When I was a kid, I used to enjoy climbing trees. I thought it was fun, and I liked the view better from up there. I still see the kids in my neighborhood occasionally climb the trees in their front yards.

Is this part of our monkey gene that all kids still have a desire to climb trees from when we were all apes and used to hunt for bananas? Is this why we eat bananas in our cereal and ice cream? If it weren't for our evolutionary history of eating bananas with everything, how would we know to mix it with cereal and ice cream? Who would have ever thought of that!!!

My question is—if we evolved from apes . . . then . . . why are there still apes?!

How can we have evolved from something that we still share the planet with?

I have been told that alligators evolved from dinosaurs. Well, do you see any dinosaurs running around! Of course not! The dinosaurs that were living at that time either died off or evolved to other creatures.

This dilemma just adds to the confusion. If we really did evolve from apes, how was it decided who shall stay and who shall go? Which apes got to stay in the jungle and swing from the vine and which apes evolved to a human and went to a nine to five job every day?

Did they just flip a coin and say, "Tommy, it looks like you are going to be a human, so we need to go shopping and find you a suit to wear to work tomorrow"?

So, now Tommy gets a new house in the burbs with a wife and two kids, and poor cousin Timmy is left in the jungle to be an ape and hunt for bananas and swing from the trees.

Or did they just pick their teams like kids do when they play a neighborhood game? One ape stood in the middle of the circle and picked his ape team. Then another ape took his turn and picked his human team.

I now feel an obligation to go out in the jungle and find my real family—my ape family. I could have a brother or sister who never had the opportunity to get picked for the human team or may have had the misfortune of getting tails in the coin toss and being left behind.

President Bush promised us "No kid would be left behind"! Where have our tax dollars been going? Why are we not helping to care for our primate relatives? I have never seen a little infant monkey in any of the daycare facilities!

I have been to my kids' school on many occasions to volunteer to read to the class, and even on career day, and I have not seen any monkey kids.

They are OUR Cousins!

I have been to the zoo many times, and I have never seen a woman breast feed a baby monkey!

We have abandoned our primate ancestors!

Why is it that when I fill out the employment application for a new job there is no category for "Ape"?

There is Hispanic, Caucasian, African American, Native Indian, and Asian. There is no category to show my true evolutionary heritage!

Next time I fill out an employment application, I will check the OTHER box and write in APE.

When I introduce myself to the *new hires* at work, I will discuss my ape family and how I miss them terribly.

I don't even know where they are. How can I find them? Why aren't they on the milk cartons?!!!

Wait a minute ... Now that I think about it ... I really do like bananas!

I usually eat one in my cereal every morning. I have even started putting bananas in my pancake batter as well. My kids often pack a banana to eat for lunch every day.

There could be some truth to this!!!

Maybe we actually volunteered to become either a human or to stay an ape. It could have been our own choice. We had free will whether or not we would go to school and work or stay in the jungle, hunt for food, and play every day.

The jungles were so overcrowded with apes, a group of them must have said, "Y'know what? There are just too many of us all competing for the same trees and the same food. Let's just split up.

"Listen up, everyone! We are going to form two different lines. In this line on the right, we need the apes who want to continue to live and play in the jungle. In the other line, we need apes to volunteer to evolve to a human. They will go to school to learn how to talk like a human and live in their self-built, human-made concrete jungle."

Obviously, if you are reading this book, you know which line you picked. I do have some days where I think, *Why did I stand in the human line? My life would have been so much easier if I'd stood in the shorter line. Why did I follow the crowd?*

Another issue only adds to my confusion. If we started out in the jungle eating a vegetarian diet of fruits and plants, when did we start eating meat? Did we get tired of eating fruits and plants, year after year, and decided one day—"I'd sure like a steak with this potato"?

Is this all part of Charles Darwin's theory of natural selection? Darwin's theory established that all species either develop traits to adapt to their current environment or eventually die off. When our environment changed to a concrete jungle devoid of many trees and plants, did we need to change our diet from a vegetarian to a meat-eater to survive and perpetuate the human race?

Or could it be that as we evolved and became more intelligent, we began to realize that every meal preparation involves another banana? "I peel it and it always tastes the same," I complained to my fellow newbies. "I have a great idea. Let's slice 'em up and make a banana cream pie for dessert!"

If Darwin's theory of adaptive evolution is true, then why are women still shaving and why are men still so darn hairy? Isn't the theory about adapting as a species to our new environment and then losing or gaining traits that are more advantageous for our new home?

We don't need hair all over our bodies! We go to the mall and buy a coat. Clothing stores have been around for many, many years. Do you really think the hair growing on your husband's back is keeping him warm on a bitterly cold day with minus seventy wind chill? "Don't worry, honey. I don't need my coat today. I grew a few more stray hairs on my back to keep me warm. I'll just wear the blue tank. It shows off my muscles better anyhow."

Why are we women still shaving our legs? We have no use for leg or underarm hair. I might as well throw that in too, while I'm at it. We don't need hairy legs anymore. We can wear pants or pantyhose.

Why haven't the humans finished evolving? Now, somebody please tell me: why did I stand in the line on the left?

This is the question our biology books should be answering. If someone wrote a book replete with scientific support and documented evidence of *Women Can Stop Shaving Their Legs—Men Can Stop Growing Back Hair: Just Evolve Naturally*, it would be a bestseller.

Let's speed up this part of our evolution. Laser hair removal is expensive and requires multiple treatments from what I've heard. According to Charles Darwin and his brilliant theory, we should have evolved to hairless leg and back "Ape Humans."

What scholar wrote these history books anyhow? I have been confused ever since elementary school. Is there anyone who verifies this information written in these research books, or is it all on the honor system?

I live in Atlanta. I'll call the Medical Department at Emory University Hospital and get to the bottom of this.

"Hey, y'all. It's Melissa, your drug rep. I met you and the rest of the staff last week during our lunch and learn. I was the one who brought in the baked chicken, mashed potatoes, green beans, sweet tea, and the yummy fudgy brownies for dessert that everyone could just die for.

"I would like to talk to your Evolution Department. I have a question regarding my family tree. I'm trying to find out if there really were apes in the tree or not."

"Oh? Sure, Melissa. We loved the chicken! It was really tender. I'll connect you."

"This is Eve in the Evolution Department. How can I help you?"

"Hi, Eve. It's Melissa, your weekly caterer. I bring in chicken. I was just wondering who wrote the very first book on our evolution from ape to human?"

"The first book was written by Dr. Brown. He is the world-renowned expert on the study of evolution."

"Dr. Brown was the first one who said we evolved from apes?" I asked to clarify.

"That's correct."

"You've got to be kidding me. I know Dr. Brown!" I exclaimed. "I brought him to a lunch that I had last week. He's ... a ... soft drink!" I yelled into the phone.

"He's a doctor ... he knows," Eve replied as she hurriedly disconnected the call.

I wanted to continue my conversation with Eve, but she hung up too quickly. I wanted to ask her if when she was in the Garden of Eden with Adam, she saw any of my ape ancestors there.

I don't remember reading in the Bible the story about Adam and Eve in the garden, playing with the apes, and fighting over the fruit and vegetables.

Did Eve eat the apple because an ape was going for it and she was hungry?

This knowledge could change our entire religious history! Why were the apes not mentioned in the Bible? Weren't they there first?

What if the story was really about Adam and Eve and the apes? Who else was in that garden?!!

Why aren't there more books on this subject? If the apes weren't there, then when did they come? How did they get here?

Did they just swing from the vines from tree to tree for thousands of miles and arrive on someone's front lawn. "Hi there! I think we're related. Do you have any bananas?"

I need to go to my local bookstore to see if there are any books written by people who remember their ape family.

Why aren't my children reading about this in school? Where are all the books from the people who remember their true ancestry? Come to think of it—I have never read an autobiography *My Childhood as an Ape*.

My family tree is incomplete. Both of my children completed a family tree for elementary school. The highest branches on the tree were their great grandparents. Who were the Mintz Apes on the branches above them?

What kind of legacy will I be leaving for my children and our future generations who have descended from the Mintz Apes if I do not try and find the missing branches on our family tree?

I guess I will have to use up all of my allotted vacation time to travel to the jungle and try to find my lost relatives. If I want something done, I'll have to do it myself—just like at home!

How will I recognize my relatives? Will I look for the closest family resemblance?

Be on the lookout for my next book. It will be a memoir titled *Finding the Mintz Apes: A Family Reunion.*

Next time y'all go to the zoo, could you please tell my Aunt Millie I said, "Hello"? She is the one in the ape exhibit eating the bananas I sent last week for her birthday.

10

Online Ordering

I really enjoy ordering clothes and other items on the computer. I can shop in the privacy of my own home. It is convenient, and I don't have to drive all over the city in the usual bumper to bumper Atlanta traffic. I am able to save on gas, save on time, and not fight anyone for the best parking space! Who cares if I find the space closest to the door! I'm shoppin' from my couch.

I can sit on my comfortable couch with my dog, Goldye, have my computer on my lap and comparison shop at many different stores in only a few minutes. I can find the best price, pay for the item, and have it shipped right to my front door. All this during a commercial break of *American Idol*.

Why miss your favorite TV show just because you need a new winter coat! That's certainly not a valid reason to get up and go out. Are you starving? Are you dehydrated from thirst? Then I can't imagine what the rush is to parade around town if you can survive with a TV remote control and a computer.

I don't even have to move. Getting up to use the bathroom requires more effort than this. I don't have to take a shower, put on makeup, change out of my lounging clothes replete with dog hair—lots of dog hair and bird poop everywhere. My pet cockatiel Spike likes to sit on my shoulder and watch me shop. He enjoys shopping and pooping, and can do both at the same time and make it all look effortless. That's my little Spikey!

I can take my time deciding what I want without dealing with pushy sales people who convincingly tell me how wonderful everything looks. Every color looks good on me … every item of clothing fits perfectly—just ask the salesperson! For everyone who tries something on, the salespeople will fawn all over you with compliments … that is … until you try to return something.

This is an evil word for retail. Have you ever noticed how nice and helpful the sales people are when you are purchasing items, and then they have a complete change of personality when you return items, especially in a store where they work on commission! At least when I return something I bought online, I just ship it back and don't have to talk to anyone to explain why I am returning it.

Sure, these are all good reasons why I would rather shop online, but it's not the real reason. I know my reason is a shared reason for all American women. We have been baffled and perplexed beyond our wildest comprehension. We have one question that has never been answered! Unless we act now, our daughters will be destined to the same fate. They will grow up, go to the mall, and have the same question. This will continue for future generations until we finally have the answer!

What is this question you might ask yourself? This is the question that we women have been asking ourselves for decades. Our own mothers have asked this question. Even our dear, sweet grandmothers had the same question.

The number one question asked by all American women regardless of race, age, or religion, is. . . .

What is the deal with the dressing room lighting???

Do they make sure they adjust the brightness to ensure that every flaw that you have ever had—and those you didn't even know you had—become visible?

No wonder why this country has so many people who have eating disorders. It's because they like to shop and can't handle the trauma of seeing themselves in an oversized dressing room mirror with bright fluorescent lighting!

Y'know what Mary-Kate Olsen was doing when she had her last meal? She was having lunch at the mall food court with Ashley, then she decided to try on a swimsuit and went into the store dressing room, took off her clothes . . . and freaked!

"Ashley . . . this swimsuit makes my butt look fat! Oh . . . my goooosh! Asshhhllleeey! My legs look like jello!!!"

Mary-Kate decided, "That's it—I'm not eating again! This dressing room makes me look FAT! I'm goin' on a liquid diet! Alcohol only! I will only eat on Tuesdays and Thursdays!"

This is what happened. I am privy to this information! This is what is happening. People all over the world have been traumatized by dressing rooms with big mirrors and superbright, unflattering fluorescent lighting.

Don't retail establishments realize how important it is that the women shoppers feel good about themselves? After all, we are the ones who contribute the most to the retail economy. It's because we care about fashion!

If women did not care about fashion, constantly shopping and buying, this country would be bankrupt. Men don't really shop—at least not in the way women do. Women usually spend hours at the mall meandering around just to see what catches their eye in the hopes of being inspired to find the perfect outfit that would look flattering on them.

Men go to the mall to play out their war fantasies of a seek and destroy mission. They are like a sniper. They know just where their target is, take care of business, and then—get out! Men's clothing is sized so much better than women's; they can find their waist and inseam size, purchase, and go.

We find an article of clothing we like and it's off to the dressing room. Why can't the dressing rooms have dim lighting? Just like the kind of lighting you would expect if you went out to a nice restaurant for dinner and the lights are turned down for a softer, more subdued look. Soft music, like smooth jazz, should be playing in the background to create an ambience of relaxation more like a spa experience in your own private, dressing room closet.

We are certainly more likely to spend money when we are relaxed and feel good about ourselves. This is basic economics 101. We don't need to be constantly reminded of our flaws and have them magnified in every funhouse style dressing room mirror.

These mirrors are like the wolf in the popular beloved children's fairy tale *Little Red Riding Hood*. They are evil, deceitful, sneaky, scary, and just BAD. Our reflection in those mirrors with fluorescent lighting magnifies all of our imperfections. The sight alone is frightful enough to bring a grown woman to tears.

Poor Mary-Kate. She didn't have a chance when she walked into that dressing room closet at the mall. Even Little Red was forewarned that the woods can be a dangerous place. By the way, is Little Red a rapper now? Just wondering. We haven't heard much from her since she was a child visiting her grandma's house.

Every dressing room should have a warning sign outside the door. They have warning signs at the entrance to ride the roller coasters at the amusement parks. When I rode Space Mountain at Disney World there was a sign that said, "If you have a pre-existing condition, DO NOT RIDE."

How about a warning sign on the outside of the dressing room?

If you have a previous history of *the uglies* in a dressing room mirror, DO NOT ENTER.

WARNING

1) Skin will look like green jiggly jello.
2) Objects in mirror will appear ten pounds heavier.
3) Your butt will be guaranteed to look big—in everything!
4) Any and all cellulite will look like New York City roads—big ugly potholes.
5) All imperfections will be magnified, which could lead to eating disorders and years of therapy!
6) If any of these things will make you cry and leave the mall in a hurry—DO NOT ENTER!

What is so difficult about putting up a sign? I can't even tell you how many times in a store I have said to the salesperson, "I'm still not sure; I think I'll buy it and try it on at home."

I used to think maybe it's just me; it's all in my head. Maybe I'm the only one who looks deformed under the scrutiny of fluorescent lights. But now I realize, I am not alone. Years of online ordering of clothes and trying them on in the privacy of my own home with nice soft lighting has cured me of "dressing room disease."

As your drug rep, I feel it is my responsibility to bring awareness to this chronic disease and help find a cure. I've got it! I just thought of a brilliant plan, and it doesn't include catering chicken to the mall! I'm going to call, Bob, the president of my pharmaceutical company and ask him to help me find a cure. "We will have a Race for the Cure!" I blurted out to Bob as we were brainstorming on a way to raise money and awareness about the hazards of dressing rooms and dressing room disease.

"We could have the race at the mall," I said, getting caught up in the excitement of my new venture. "Race past Sears and Victoria's Secret and Macy's." I rambled on with my racing thoughts, and then continued, "The temperature is controlled, and the shoppers could participate as the spectators cheering on the participants.

"And you know what else, Bob?" I said, realizing by now that I really didn't need his help at all. "The employees from Auntie Anne's Pretzels could set up a table of small cups of Orange Julius for the racers as they pass.

"Gosh Bob, I'm so good at these party planning events! I'd pat myself on the back, but my shoulders are still sore from leaning against the wall all day."

My hope was that after the big race, we would finally have enough money to cure the disease. We will buy a new 40-watt soft white light bulb for every dressing room in the country!

This is it! I thought. Women all over the country will finally find relief from this disfiguring dressing room disease.

Unfortunately, we found out after the race, not every store in America was willing to replace their fluorescent light bulbs with the new soft white lighting. There were still millions of women who were suffering.

I know! I have another plan. These days, there is a pill for everything! I'll call Bob again and ask him to work with the research department to develop a pill for the prevention of dressing room disease.

Bob came through again. The research department decided to put the drug on a fast track for production to be on the market in just a few weeks! They already have a huge marketing campaign with ads in all the medical journals and even a television commercial.

This is so exciting! The new drug will be called "Magic Mirror," and it is indicated for the prevention of dressing room disease.

I just saw the 30-second commercial for the new Magic Mirror pill and thought it was very well done. It went like this. . . .

There is a forty-something woman standing in a dressing room admiring the way she looks in an orange, polka dot, one-piece swimsuit in the brightly lit, florescent, three-way mirror. She is smiling and looks so happy despite the fact that her skin looks like ripply, green, jiggly jello in her reflection.

During this scene, the announcer is stating the side effects in the background.

"The side effects of Magic Mirror, once a day pill for dressing room disease, include: weight gain, butt sweat, excessive upper lip hair, walking farts, and an uncontrollable craving for chocolate. Ask your doctor about Magic Mirror once-a-day pill. Please take as directed for a lifetime of tear-free shopping."

Wow!!! I have to tell y'all, I was so moved by this commercial. It just about brought me to tears. Just knowing that I had something to do with helping so many of these women having a better quality of life is enough gratitude to make all of those days of schlepping in cookies, cakes, and donuts in the freezing cold torrential rain so worthwhile. I will never complain about my job again! I just decided.

Women all over the country will be begging their doctors to prescribe Magic Mirror. My sales will go through the roof!

Who would have ever thought a drug rep could change the world?!

I am so proud of myself! Wait till I tell my kids what I did—they'll be proud of me, too. I'll finally get the respect that I deserve! By the way, does anyone have some pain pills? My shoulder still hurts. Anyhow. . . .

11

Chocolate

I took my kids to a museum here in Atlanta because they had a chocolate exhibit. The exhibit was about the history of chocolate. They showed how chocolate was made and the many different uses of chocolate throughout history.

Cacao beans were first used by the Aztecs and the Mayans to make a hot, frothy drink, mixed with various spices that were very bitter. They would roast the cocoa seeds, grind them into a paste with a stone, add water and spices, and drink it like we would drink hot chocolate; only they didn't have sugar to add to make it taste sweet. It wasn't until 1876 that we had the chocolate we enjoy today with milk, cocoa powder, sugar, and cocoa butter.

I consider chocolate to be one of life's best inventions.

Who would have thought that adding some sugar to bitter cacao beans would be such a delectable food? I eat chocolate almost every day. When I wake up in the morning, I look forward to starting off my day with a piece of velvety, rich chocolate to awaken my senses.

I prefer to eat a piece of chocolate with my breakfast so I can start my day with the most important food group. Scrambled eggs and a piece of chocolate—now that's a breakfast for champions! Some mornings I will have dark chocolate and other mornings I'll gobble the milk chocolate. I am not a picky chocolate fancier. I like dark, milk, and white chocolate. Chocolate is definitely at the top of my food pyramid!

I like it on fruit, especially strawberries and bananas. I like chocolate pie and chocolate cake; and like most people I know, I love a good brownie. I would probably even like it on my meatloaf—as a glaze. I think I'll try it next time. Instead of reaching for the ketchup bottle, I'll just drizzle some melted chocolate on top. The kids will love it! Mom's homemade chocolate-glazed meatloaf. Dessert and an entrée—all in one bite.

The kids are always saying, "You make the same stuff all the time! We're tired of eating grilled chicken!" I really should try and experiment with more recipes and add chocolate. The problem is, when I do make a concerted effort to cook a gourmet meal and try out a new recipe, the kids say they hate it and refuse to eat. My time in preparation and the food just goes to waste.

I know they like chocolate so much, in fact, that when I buy some for myself as a treat, they snarf it down and leave me with none. I have resorted to hiding it from them. On the way home from work today, I stopped at Barnes and Noble to buy a book. As I was in line at the checkout counter, I noticed a Godiva chocolate stand. I recognized their signature gold boxes, and I was already starting to drool. It has become a conditioned reflex for me. I see the gold box and turn into one of Pavlov's dogs.

I have to have it! I'll buy myself a little gift, I heard my own voice rationalize this purchase inside my head. I picked out a box of milk and dark chocolate truffles, and knew as soon as I got into the privacy of my car I was going to rip off the gold paper and eat two: one dark chocolate and one milk chocolate, to sample of course.

As I usually do, since I am a good mom, I decided I would share with the kids when I got home. "You each get one!" I said in my best authoritative voice. "I bought it for me. It's my gift!" They each stuffed a piece in their mouth and did what they always do—begged for more.

So I did what any sane and sensible mom in this position would do. "I touched the rest of them and breathed on all of them, so now they're all mine!" I yelled. "I may cough on them later, too. You won't know if I did or not, so don't *even* try to find my hiding place!"

As soon as I said this, I realized I am turning into a loon. *I am turning into them,* I thought to myself. I hear my kids declare the good food and snacks by doing gross stuff all the time. "Nobody better touch the leftover Thai food— it's all mine!" I have heard my son Brandon say. "I already sneezed all over it!"

"I already drank out of the sweet tea," they'll say to claim their favorite drink with the threat of backwash and slobber.

Sometimes the food may even have a note attached, just in case you forget; I guess. "I touched all of it and my hands were dirty. Love, Morgan."

Hmmmm . . . we really can learn from our kids, I thought, as I was rushing up the steps to my room to find an appropriate hiding place for my beloved gold box.

Chocolate makes me happy!

I like everything about it. I like the taste. I like how it melts in my mouth. I like the aroma of chocolate, and I just like to look at it.

Chocolate looks even better when you view it in a store through the glass case. I like looking at the trays of the milk chocolate and dark chocolate, and try to imagine how all the distinctive shapes with different fillings would taste.

I especially like it when the pieces have pretty designs with a beautiful mixture of dark and milk chocolate. When I walk into a chocolate store, I am in heaven. I can't wait to taste all the beautiful creations of the different *chocolate works of art.*

I have often wondered, *Why did Picasso paint? He could have created beautiful artistic chocolates. Such a waste of his talent!*

Chocolate also contains a chemical PEA (phenylethyl-amine). This is the same chemical that is released when we are in love.

Chocolate is the food of love.

When we are falling in love, our brain releases even more of this chemical. This may be why chocolate is the gift of choice on Valentine's Day. Giving a gift of chocolate suggests romance and seduction. Chocolate is very sensual. With its rich, sweet, velvety taste and smooth creamy texture, chocolate seduces the senses and makes you want more.

Chocolate is the Michael Phelps of candy. It is in a league of its own. There is no other candy like chocolate. It has been around for over a hundred years and, thank goodness, it's here to stay.

"Hey Michael, have you tried scrambled eggs and chocolate before you race?" Protein and carbs—perfect for a champion! In the next Olympics you can thank me from the podium; just wave, and I'll know it's meant for me.

I think everyone should love chocolate. I just can't understand someone not liking chocolate. I can understand a person not liking licorice, gummy bears, or even caramel ... but ... chocolate? That's just plain ... well ... weird! I can understand if it's a food allergy, sort of; but quite honestly, I don't trust people who don't like chocolate.

There are two types of people I do not trust. I don't trust people who don't eat chocolate, and I don't trust people who dislike animals.

What kind of person doesn't like a loyal doggie that loves us unconditionally and is always so happy to see us when we walk through the door?

Who wouldn't like a cute, little, furry, hoppity bunny rabbit with their adorable white cotton ball tail?

I'll tell you who—and they don't eat chocolate!

It's a well documented fact that more women than men crave chocolate. Chocolate is the number one food craved by women in America, especially during that "time of the month." There have been many theories on why this occurs. Some researchers have attributed this craving to the high magnesium content in chocolate. Others have thought it may be due to the increase in serotonin (the feel good hormone) by eating chocolate.

Who . . . cares . . . why?! All women need chocolate!

Women no longer send the men in their life out for a 3:00 a.m. tampon run. They send their man out for a chocolate run. "Come back with chocolate or don't come back at all," they scream and throw a shoe at his back as he is running out the door. Glad to escape the *hormonal house of horror,* the poor guy complies and runs out to the nearest 24-hour pharmacy. This is the reason that pharmacies have now become our candy stores!

They have every type of candy imaginable. There are rows of candy bars and beautifully wrapped candy boxes full of delectable fine chocolates filled with cream fillings, fruits, and nuts. There is an entire candy aisle in addition to the candy located by the checkout counter in case you are really in a hurry and don't have time to browse.

The pharmacists got tired of hearing men pleading for candy bars in the middle of the night and decided there was an unmet need to supply 24-hour chocolate.

I crave chocolate too, but I crave chocolate every day. I really think it may be addictive. If I don't have my chocolate for breakfast, I can get a little cranky.

There are two things I want in life. I want world peace, and I want chocolate!

Whenever I watch the *Miss America Pageant* on TV, the majority of the women mention something about wanting world peace. Liars! Why don't they tell the truth? They want chocolate! They are hoping for world peace, and it sounds better on national television than telling the truth. "I am craving chocolate and I want some—NOW! Also, I hope someday we have world peace."

In addition to learning about the history of chocolate at the museum, there was a chocolate exhibit on the main floor where we were able to sample chocolate from the different vendors who participated and brought their goodies for us to eat. They had samples of different types of chocolate: dark, milk, and white chocolate, and even chocolate ice cream.

The entrance fee to the museum included the chocolate exhibit of free samples. There were huge lines for the free samples that had lines of people circling around the main floor. There were people everywhere in all the different lines for each sample table.

There were lines for the ice cream. There were lines to sample each different type of chocolate. It was difficult to tell where one line started and another line ended. We just stood in an end of a line not knowing what was at the other end, mostly because we could not see the end. We were just walking in circles until we finally got to the table with the chocolate goodies.

I stood in a line with the kids for thirty minutes to get a little piece of chocolate from a block of chocolate that I have seen before at the grocery store on a table where the baked goods are sold.

As a matter of fact, all of the chocolate and the ice cream were the same brands we can buy at any time from the local grocery. I've seen that same chocolate and ice cream every time I go to the grocery store. Have I ever thought even one time that I wanted to buy it—no! But I will stand in a circle line for twenty to thirty minutes for each item to get a free sample.

I was starting to feel ridiculous going from one long line to another in this packed main floor of the museum. It was like Oliver meets Willy Wonka. "Please sir, can I have more chocolate?"

I wanted to leave, but the kids wanted to stay. "I'll take you to the grocery store and buy you that same chocolate. There's no line!" I said, trying to reason with them.

"But Mom . . . it's free!" they both chimed in.

It drives me nuts when I hear that something is free. Just the other day when I pulled up to a popular drive-thru coffee restaurant the cashier asked, "Would you like your coffee for free today?"

"Sure I would!" I replied, thinking it must be my lucky day. Maybe I am the 100th car that pulled up this morning, and I won a cup of coffee as my prize. *Just my luck,* I thought to myself. Some people when they are lucky win the lottery with a multi-million dollar cash prize, and all I win is a free cup of the coffee of the day for a total value of $2.

Just as I was contemplating my luck, I was interrupted by the cashier, "That's great ma'am . . . all you have to do is buy this five-pound bag of our original roast coffee and we'll give you a cup for free!"

"I guess I'll pay!" I replied, thinking how gullible I must be.

"Free!" I exclaimed to the kids. "I paid at least $40 for all of us to see this exhibit. I'm sure that covered our share of the 'free samples'!"

The kids won as they usually do. I stood in every line for a total of an hour and a half to eat my free $40 worth of chocolate samples.

I hope you enjoy my writing. It's free. It was included in the book.

12

Party City

L iving in a neighborhood is like being back in high school. Everyone seems to always know what you are up to and if they don't know, they will just make some stuff up. They now take this newfound knowledge and pass this worthless information on to the rest of the neighbors to keep everyone in the loop of what is going on in their community. It is like you are living in a goldfish bowl where everyone seems to want to peer in and see what you are doing all the time.

When you purchase your home you are now part of your free Neighborhood Country Club. Family membership starts as soon as you close on your new home. Since you are now new members of the club, your address and telephone number are published in the monthly neighborhood newsletter to guarantee you're welcomed by all of the existing residents.

Our welcome letters seem to come immediately after we move in. Unfortunately, this is not in the form of, "Hi, my name is so and so. If you ever need anyone to water your plants or take in your mail while you are on vacation, please call me. I would be glad to help." The welcome letters are now invitations to parties, parties, and more parties! Your new neighborhood is like Party City.

Most people would assume this Neighborhood Country Club membership would include unlimited golf use, and access to the swimming pool and tennis courts. Well, not in my 'hood. This free membership includes invitations to every Tupperware party, jewelry party, sex toy party, Pampered Chef party, woven basket party, and any other party where you are expected to purchase items for your personal or decorating needs.

When I was in college, a party was associated with loud music, great food, beer, wine, and other party beverages, along with fun, interesting people. *All of a sudden, a party is associated with bringing your checkbook to the neighbor's house!* Just attending the party becomes an obligation to purchase an item in the party book of items for sale.

I have been to many of these neighborhood parties since I have lived in my house. The most recent party that I attended was from a neighbor down the street who had a basket party. I was hoping to dodge the party, but when she personally called due to my lack of an RSVP, I could not think of an excuse quick enough and was roped into attending.

It does not matter what type of neighborhood party you are invited to; the format is essentially the same for all of them. The party decorations usually consist of some kind of homemade, unrecognizable appetizer on the kitchen table along with assorted opened soft drinks that you're sure their kids already drank out of the containers!

As we enter the house, we are herded to the two rooms where the guests will congregate. This is usually the kitchen and family room, since these are the rooms that were cleaned enough to look presentable before the neighbors arrived. We then mingle with the same neighbors we have painstakingly tried to avoid all day!

After a brief reception around the kitchen table, which consists of a cursory "Hello" over a plastic cup of the fizzless orange soda, we are led into the family room to take our seat for the initial presentation that starts off this shindig. The good seats, like the couch and recliner, fill up first leaving the card table style, cheap, folding metal chairs for myself and others less fortunate.

The host of the party, who has been incentivized by the free party gift, now becomes a walking talking infomercial. "These baskets are the most durable baskets ever made!" I hear our hostess proclaim as I am chugging the bottled water I hid in my purse. After our hostess finishes her presentation, we are then asked to each take a turn to discuss the basket we like the most and how we plan on using it. This is done to create enthusiasm and excitement over the new opportunities presented before us.

To help get things started, our hostess decides to go around the room so that each of us gets a chance to talk. Since this is a basket party, there are many assorted baskets in different shapes and sizes scattered about the room so we could actually see the samples available to purchase. And of course, being passed around is the party book catalogue of baskets so that we could place additional orders for all our decorating or gift-giving needs.

"So, Carole," the hostess says, obviously starting clockwise in the circle, "which basket was your favorite?"

"I think I liked the large basket with the curved handle for carrying."

"What great taste you have! That's my favorite, too!" coos our hostess as if hoping we might be catching on that we were there to actually purchase something.

"Can you tell everyone how you think you would use it, Carole?"

"Ummmm ... let's see. ... " I could tell Carole is stalling for time to think of a suggestion for usage of a basket that she had—in the mind of the hostess—verbally committed to buying with her previous praise of *I think I liked it* in front of witnesses.

Shirley chimes in for her rescue. "Carole, that basket would look nice in your guest bathroom. Y'know," she continues, "you could keep your purple and gold hand towels in there—roll them up real pretty and stack them in there all fancy."

This teamwork is really good, I think. No one wants to be put on the spot.

Shirley looks around the room and smiles, knowing she now has the floor. "You could keep a roll of toilet paper on top for convenience in case the roll on the holder runs out while readin' *Southern Living*. I just hate when that happens! Then you've got to get up and scoot around the house lookin' for some paper with your pants around your ankles." Shirley stands up to act this scene out as if we are now playing charades.

I really enjoy live theater, I think to myself. Maybe I'll act out my comment as well. At least the party is becoming somewhat entertaining.

"Elaine, it's your turn," the hostess chimes in to keep the conversation moving to the next future basket owner.

"Okay ... I'm going to purchase the square basket for my daughter's Beanie Babies. Those things are all over the floor. She must have a hundred of those stupid things. We paid a fortune for some of those Beanies—told they would be collectors' items and all. Collectors' items! ... Oh give me a break! There's dog slobber on most of them. My adorable little white toy poodle Gucci thinks they're her doggie toys. Every time I look at that dog, she has a rabbit or duck or monkey in her mouth. Last night, she was gnawing on the Princess Diana Beanie Bear that cost me fifty dollars to get in 1997. Maybe if my daughter cleaned her room once in a. ... "

"Okay, great! Thank you, Elaine," our hostess with the mostess finally breaks the impending diatribe.

Jacqueline just can't keep quiet any longer. "I know I'm expected to purchase something, but I really need to get home and give my twins a bath. Here's ten dollars. Just put me down for the cheapest thing in the book."

That was brilliant!!! Why didn't I think of something like that? I feel just a little envious that she got to make her great escape. Now, there's someone I could be friends with. I make a mental note to invite her to lunch next week.

"By the way, I think your appetizer gave me diarrhea!" she yells as she hurries out the door.

As we continue around the room, a few other suggestions are mentioned. "I'll get one for the remote control for the TV."

"Me too!" yell a couple of women, feeling relieved they only had to say two words to end their turn.

Helen Sue is sitting next to me, and I am sitting in the last chair in the circle by the hostess. "How much is that big one in the corner?" she asks. "Maybe I'll buy it and stuff a fake tree in there. My dog keeps peeing on the real one we have. Better there than the carpet, I suppose," she says with a sigh of relief that her dog has a proclivity for nature instead of synthetic materials.

"That's a good idea, Helen Sue!" Nicole and Lynn say in unison, as if suddenly concerned their apathy might be noticeable. "Fake flowers might look good, too," Nicole continues, as if helping Helen Sue with other choices her dog might like to pee on.

All of us are trying to sound enthused about buying something we really could give a crap about. The acting ability here is equivalent to the *Kelly Loves Justin* movie from the first season of *American Idol*.

As the evening winds down, a few of the partygoers become more interested in gossiping about neighbors who weren't in attendance than continuing to watch this poorly performed neighborhood production of *Why I Love My Basket*.

Several of the attendees had moved over to the kitchen table to refill their empty plastic cups that are still warm from being in the dishwasher.

"Who re-uses plastic cups?" I want to ask, only to realize I already had my answer. The same people who serve two large bottles of already opened generic orange soda that lost its fizz a week ago.

I look at my watch, wondering how much more I would have to endure. I have been there for two hours. Surely these festivities would end soon. This is definitely the last party I'm going to, I decide.

"Well, Melissa, what will you be purchasing tonight?" is finally my lead in by the party hostess to talk. *Asking a salesperson if they would like to talk is like asking a toilet if it's ever seen pee!* There's nothing a sales person loves more than a captive audience. I enjoy talking; after all, that's what I get paid to do every day.

It's finally my turn to talk, and I open with, "I think I like the small woven basket with the pretty burgundy flower lining. It might look okay in the kitchen, although I may have to change the kitchen wallpaper so the cloth lining in the basket doesn't clash with the decor.

"No problem," I continue to say. "I'm sure I can redecorate my house to make sure the twenty dollar palm-sized basket can feel at home," I finish, trying to soften the hint of sarcasm.

"Share with all of us how you will use the basket?" is my next question from the party hostess.

During this question I have a flashback of my kindergarten show-and-tell days. Of course, our infomercial party hostess is hoping that my suggestion may convince the other neighbors that they, too, should have to redecorate their house as well to find space for this important decorating item with many practical uses.

"I will put it on the desk in the kitchen and place my car keys in it after each drive to make sure I know where they are. I can never find my car keys, y'know ... takes me foreeeeveeer to find!"

"What a wonderful idea!!!" the party hostess squeals with delight! "Did everyone hear how Melissa is going to use her new basket? Does anyone else misplace their car keys? Raise your hand!"

I sell twelve baskets this evening for the party hostess with my practical suggestion for the little woven basket. As most of us hand in our order form to the hostess, the other members of the group are tripping over each other running out the door muttering, "Have to say goodnight to the little ones before they go to sleep."

A few of the regular partiers hang around to see who got the backwash from the soda bottle before they call it a night.

We can never seem to escape from all of the partying going on! Don't think you are off the hook if you happen to have other plans or if you are the lucky ones who can fit both cars in your garage so no one knows if you are really home or not.

They will come—they will track you down—they will find you.

The following day, you will be guaranteed to have a knock on your door with the party book in hand from the evening's infomercial hostess stating, "I am so sorry you missed the party. We had sooooo much fun. I know you wanted to order something, so please fill out your order form and return it to me as soon as possible so I can turn all the orders in together."

What this really means is *I might be ten dollars short for qualifying for my free party hostess gift,* so you better order something pronto!

I used up all of my kids' soda at the party!

I want a return on my investment!!!

To this day, I still have my small woven basket with the burgundy flower lining on my kitchen desk. When I actually do find my car keys, this is where I place them.

Now, if only I could find the basket.

"Hey kids! Where's the basket! Did anyone see where the basket went? I need my car keys! Kiiiidddddddsssss ... !!!! Hey, Brandon, did you see the basket?"

"Nope. Morgan probably did it."

"Morgan ... what about you ... ?"

"Brandon's the one who moves everything!" she screamed, as if falsely accused again.

This is why in China they only have one kid. They always know who moved the basket!

13

Fast Food

Everyone seems to be so busy now that we are all in a hurry to get somewhere. Get home—get to work—get the kids to soccer practice—get to the grocery store. . . . When we want to eat, there is no time. We want everything NOW!

There is so little time to cook these days, as now more families have both parents working to pay the bills. When dinnertime comes around, there is little time to prepare a healthy home-cooked meal. For many families, dinnertime is usually fast-food or frozen food cooked in the microwave oven.

Kids these days are so used to eating fast-food that they don't even like home-cooked meals. They think the food tastes weird. You will even hear kids talking about whether something tastes good on how closely it resembles their favorite fast-food. "WOW! Mom, this taco tastes pretty good. It tastes almost like

Taco Bell!" Fast-food has now become the gold standard for a child's palate.

When I make a hamburger for my kids, I smash the burgers with a spatula while they are cooking to make sure they are really flat. Kids don't like fat and juicy hamburgers. They want their home-cooked burgers to taste more like thin, pancake-style, fast-food burgers.

If your kid says, "Dinner was great tonight, Mom. The burgers tasted just like McDonald's!" they are giving you their highest praise for a home-cooked meal. This compliment is the kiddie version of five stars.

We are now using fresh ingredients to make our home-cooked meals taste more like fast-food so our youngsters will actually sit down and eat a meal.

My son had a friend over from school to do homework together, and I was cooking dinner, hamburgers and fries when I received a phone call from his mom.

"Billy will only eat fast-food. I will go through a drive-thru and be over shortly with his dinner," she explained.

"I'm grilling hamburgers and cooking fries in the fryer just like the fast-food places do. Will you eat this?" I pleaded with Billy to save his mom a trip over to the house.

"Nope," said Billy, "I will only eat fast-food hamburgers and fast-food fries!"

This kid will probably be featured in Michael Moore's next documentary *Fast-Food Junkie*. They will document his treatment program as he is weaned off his fast-food addiction in his padded room, pleading for a McDonald's cheeseburger to stave off the tremors and hallucinations.

Even in the area where I live, the fast-food restaurants are always crowded. There is always a line at the drive-thru to place your order. I really do try to make a genuine effort to prepare a home-cooked meal for my kids, but there are times when they are screaming, "We're starving!" I give in and take them through a drive-thru.

It just seems so bizarre to go through a fast-food drive-thru while already eating another fast-food item. I feel like a disgusting glutton. Brandon called me while Morgan and I were in the car eating a McDonald's ice cream cone dipped in chocolate. "Go to Zaxby's and bring me home some boneless chicken wings and fries!" he demanded.

"You have to wait until Morgan and I have finished our ice cream cone! I can't go through Zaxby's drive-thru licking an ice cream cone while waiting for your wings, fries, cole slaw, garlic toast, and your chocolate chip cookie."

"But, I'm starving!" he whined.

"Morgan and I are in Zaxby's parking lot finishing our ice cream cone! I am not going to be slobbering on this ice cream cone while I'm waiting for your order ... I live here for God's sake! What will people think, that I go from one fast-food restaurant to another and stuff my face?

"There's a rule, Brandon," I continued, "You have to finish one fast-food item before you can order another one. That's the fast-food rule, and I'm sticking to it. So you'll just have to wait about thirty minutes until we're home with your food!"

When I was a kid there was only one window—not two—for the *drive-thru*. When you pulled your car up, you paid at the same window your received your food. Most people would think the reason why there are now two windows is to increase efficiency. We pay at the first window, then pull up and grab our food at the second window. This is not the reason. The reason why you pay first is because if you have ever spent a lot of time looking through the window watching the workers prepare your food, you would be so grossed out that you would leave before you paid!

I know this for a fact, because I used to peer through the window while I was waiting for my food and became so disgusted I would just drive off. They didn't have my money yet! I wasn't financially obligated to wait for my food!

I used to pull an ORDER and RUN.

I have seen workers sneeze on my food, cough on my food, wipe the snot from their nose with their hands and then grab the bun, play with their hair, and even eat a few of the fries from my order as it was being passed to the worker at the window.

I was at a Dairy Queen drive-thru getting ready to hand over my cash in exchange for my small vanilla cone dipped in chocolate, when I saw the guy's hand bleeding from a cut.

There was new blood and dried blood all over his hand. This was a no-brainer. I pulled back the hand with my money very quickly and drove off. I hope he enjoyed my ice cream!

Nowadays, many of the workers preparing the food wear gloves. I really like the gloves if they are used appropriately. As a matter of fact, the only reason why I occasionally go to Subway with the kids is because the workers put on a fresh pair of gloves before they make each sandwich, and I don't have to be grossed out from them touching my food.

Sometimes, the gloves are used inappropriately. For instance, I was at a grocery store deli counter waiting to order my weekly supply of sliced turkey breast for the kids' school lunches. The deli worker saw me and hollered, "Be right with you!"

I watched him wear his gloves while he finished sweeping the floor and collected the dirty garbage to take out later. Finally, he completed his chores and came over to slice my pound of turkey.

I kept watching him, thinking, *Surely he is going to take off his gloves and put on a fresh new pair!* Nope, never happened. I realized these are the same pair of gloves he had on all day. *He probably went to the bathroom with his gloves on.* Do you really think my turkey made it to the checkout line? Ha!

It's as though the workers in the food industry think that gloves are worn to protect their hands from germs instead of our food. "Good thing I have these gloves on while I'm cleaning out the sink, taking out the trash, and cleaning up the vomit on aisle three. Thanks for waiting. I'm ready to make your turkey sandwich now. Thank goodness for these gloves. My hands feel so soft— like a baby's bottom!"

I have seen signs in restaurant bathrooms that say, "Employees must wash hands." I think we need to add a sign that says, "Employees must take off gloves before they wipe." If you think your food tastes like shit, you may be right!

The most disgusting thing I have seen was in a local meat store near my house where they have freshly cut meat and sell a few condiments such as meat sauces and marinades. It was during flu season, and the guy working there obviously had a very bad cold. This was my first time in the store, and I was ready to purchase a freshly-cut brisket for dinner that night, and possibly buy one of their marinades for that special touch of flavor.

As I was standing in front of the beautiful array of the many different cuts of fresh meat behind the glass case, I heard a very loud sneeze. I abruptly looked up to see the man working there helping the lady next to me pick out a couple of steaks.

He sneezed again, even louder this time, and took his gloved hand to wipe his nose. He then moved his hand to pick up the steak, which elongated the visible string of snot from his nose that had adhered to his glove.

The snot on his glove was now visible and you could actually see the snot on the bright red steak. His nose was still dripping as he moved his hand from the raw steak to his nose to repeatedly wipe. I stood there in horror thinking to myself, *Is this lady crazy? She is watching this and is going to put this on the grill to feed to her loving family!*

I didn't even see this item served on the reality show *Fear Factor*. "Okay everyone, to stay in the competition, you have to eat steak marinated in snot."

Could this have been the cause of the vomit on aisle three of the grocery store? "I'm so sorry, sir," she cried, "I hardly ever puke in public, but I saw the grossest thing at the meat store around the corner!"

I was still in my reverie, trying to comprehend what I was seeing, when I heard the lady standing next to me finally speak up. "Could you take off your gloves and put on a new pair?" she exclaimed with a controlled anger to her voice.

I left the meat store and have never returned, still haunted by the snotty steak. Chick-fil-A says it best: "Eat mor chikin."

My kids just came home from school. They opened the door and yelled, "We're starvin'!"

Hey … Does Taco Bell deliver?

14

Information Technology (IT)

When I was growing up, our house had two forms of what I considered new technology. We had an intercom system throughout the house and a working gas grill installed directly into the kitchen countertop. We were the only house of everyone I knew with this cool technology. The intercom system had the main unit in the kitchen near the small desk where the phone was mounted to the wall. We did not even have a cordless phone. It was not until I was in high school when we had a cordless, so if you talked on the phone you were sitting next to wherever it was installed in your house.

The best thing about having the phone mounted on the wall is you always knew where it was. Now I hear the phone ring, I don't answer it! I can't find the phone— EVER. It doesn't matter that we have four cordless phones throughout the house. They are nowhere to be found. I think the majority of the phones are somewhere in Morgan's room hidden under a pile of clothes.

I get tired of chasing the ring only to run out of time and have the answering machine pick up. This would make for a great televised game show. Hey, Ellen DeGeneres! I have a new game for your show. Find the ringing phone before the answering machine comes on.

In my childhood home, the intercom system had a satellite unit in each room of the house mounted to the wall. It looked like a small square box with a speaker and a lever to move to talk or listen.

I am not sure what my parents were thinking when they installed the intercom system as they built the house. Did they expect that we would all communicate in an efficient and quiet manner if we needed to talk to someone? I think their original plan was that we would walk to the intercom system located in each room and move the lever to talk.

Apparently, this required just too much effort. I honestly cannot remember one time that we used the intercom system to talk to each other in the house. As a family, we communicated the old-fashioned way. We yelled and screamed as loud as we could throughout the house.

These days things are much different. Almost all kids have cell phones. It's a necessity in our busy lifestyle. Both of my kids have a cell phone. I feel better knowing they have a phone in case of an emergency and that I am able to reach them at all times.

My kids don't scream for me in the house — they call me on their cell phone!

All of a sudden my cell phone will ring and Morgan will say, "Mom, where are you?"

"I am in the laundry room. Where are you?" I yell into the phone.

One time, while sitting on the couch together watching TV, I say, "Morgan, I want to ask you something."

"Call me on my cell phone!"

"Are you kidding me? You're right next to me!!!" I shout. We still yell throughout the house, just on our cell phones. Ridiculous!

I decided I might as well go with the flow, so now I have two choices. I can scream throughout the house for the kids or call them on their cell phones. "Dinner's ready. Come in the kitchen NOW, before everything gets cold," I calmly say when I talk to Morgan and Brandon on their respective cell phones.

As a kid, I soon came to realize the intercom system had one real purpose, and that was to talk on it as loudly as I could when my parents locked me in my room for a time-out. Although I was never in a time-out for more than a few minutes, I used to get on the intercom and holler, "Let me out!!!! Let me out!!!!" until my dad would open the door and come into my room to ask me to calm down.

My plan always worked. The door was opened and I made my great escape to the family room where the TV was. That's another thing that was different back then. People did not have a TV in every room like they do now; it was considered more of a luxury item. There was usually one television set located in the family room or TV room.

We didn't have cable, so our stations consisted of about eight channels that you would change with the manual dial on the front of the television set. The kids were the only remote controls. My dad used to say, "Get up and change the channel to eight." This is how I grew up. My technology training consisted of how to dial a rotary phone mounted on the wall and change the dial on a TV set to eight different stations.

No wonder my kids think I am a complete idiot!!!

It certainly doesn't help that these reality shows only reinforce how stupid adults actually are. My kids turn on the TV and hear a grown-up proclaim, "My name is Bill Smith. I am NOT smarter than a fifth grader!" No wonder none of the kids today even bother to listen to their parents after the fourth grade.

I don't understand the premise of this show at all. If in season one we have already established that adults are not smarter than fifth graders, you would think that season two would be with fourth graders. Season three would be with third graders and so on, until we have finally found a grade level where the parents can actually win.

If we establish for an entire season that none of the grownups are smarter than a fifth grader, why are we still playing against them? Why aren't we competing against children who are more academically age appropriate to finally give the adults a chance, like "Are you smarter than a preschooler?"

Jeff Foxworthy can ask the classroom of little kids a question while they are sitting on their Fisher-Price potties learning to use the toilet. The sad reality is that, while these preschoolers are learning to wipe their own butt, they can still kick ours in any question relating to computers, video games, and technology!

I know this may sound crazy. It may even seem a little *out there,* but don't we want the rest of the world to think we are smart? What kind of a country are we? Bragging on national television about being stupider than a fifth grader?

The Japanese must be looking at us thinking, *No wonder the Americans didn't invent the Wii.* It was actually invented by a Japanese kid in the sixth grade at Wii Foo Yung Chop Suey Elementary during recess. Hence, the name Wii for short.

The kids were taking a short break from working on their invention of the first fully transplantable robotic brain and decided they wanted to play a game of baseball, but they didn't have the proper accoutrements, no bats, gloves—not even a baseball. This was the start of the brainchild of this cool new technology.

I do remind my kids from time to time that I did go to college and have a degree! "I aced Nuclear Physics!" I would say as I begged my son, Brandon, to load some music on my iPod.

Even when I was in college, the hip new technology that was a must have to do schoolwork on was a word processor. This was similar to Word on our computers today. You could type and make changes instead of using a typewriter where mistakes were difficult and messy to erase by using white-out and typing over it.

Now all of a sudden, I am expected to be an IT (Information Technology) expert on every newfangled gadget that comes on the market.

I admit, I like some of the new technology that can help make our lives easier and is simple enough to use so I don't have to spend any time reading the directions. I absolutely love my GPS. I have one in my car that I place on the windshield. Now, this is technology that really makes my life easier. Before the GPS, I used to print directions from MapQuest every day to travel from one doctor's office to another to avoid the highway traffic and stay on the back roads. I love that I don't have to think so much when I drive. Now I can focus on more important things like eating my lunch on my lap or listening to my favorite radio station.

I also like the new technology of swiping my credit card. It's so much easier than giving your credit card to the cashier. At least when I swipe the card, I know where it is. I don't have to worry about the cashier remembering to give it back. Whoever invented the question "Do you need cash back?" on that machine is a genius. Yes . . . I do!

All the other technology is just too confusing and overwhelming for me. I feel like I don't have the time to keep up with all the changes. I was just getting the hang of how to use my portable CD player when they came out with iPods and MP3 players. I have no idea how these work and how to get the songs transferred to my MP3. I don't even know what iPod and MP3 mean. I don't want to know. I don't have any more space in my brain to remember what it is.

I can barely figure out all the applications on the computer I am writing on. We did not have computer training when I was in school. My computer training was at my second pharmaceutical job out of college. We were trained on using email and how to record our physician sales calls at the end of the day. These days, computer training is FREE. All you have to do is put some cookies in the oven and invite a neighborhood kid to come over. "Honey, I just baked some fresh cookies. Ask your mommy if you can come over and play with my new computer!" Not only can the kid set up the computer to your wireless network and printer (without reading directions), but they are a whiz at PowerPoint and can even show you how to adopt a pet on Webkinz. This is a computer game my nephews Tyler and Chase love to play. You adopt a pet and play computer games to earn points to feed the pet and furnish the pet's house.

I was so proud of myself. I recently bought a new computer and printer, and was worried that I would have to hire a computer expert from either the Geek Squad or Nerds in a Flash to come to the house to set everything up. First of all, why are those mobile IT workers called geeks and nerds? That makes me feel even dumber! I have to hire a geek or a nerd to come over to my house to assist me. I actually amazed myself that I was able to connect my computer to my wireless Internet and email account.

I called my mom to share the good news. "Mom!" I said, quite pleased with myself, "I probably saved about $150 by not having a geek or a nerd come to the house and set up all of my computer stuff! Isn't that great?" I said excitedly, hoping she would share in the acknowledgement of my brilliance.

"Well, nowadays it's a lot easier to set all that stuff up," she replied, not sounding very impressed. "Everything is color-coded."

"Color-coded?" I exclaimed, "What do you mean ... color-coded?!"

"You know, they have a color on the printer and you plug the same color into your computer. They give you a color for your email that you plug in another color-coded hole in your computer," she replied casually.

"Mom, this isn't color by number," I said, disappointed that she did not acknowledge my accomplishment. "What are you talking about?" I said again, still confused, "I didn't use any colors to set up my computer!"

Then she replied, "Y'know, the cable guy was just here to fix the cable. I didn't even know I was already set up for the 'higher dimension' channels."

Now, I understand why my kids think I am an idiot. "By the way, Mom," I replied, "it's High Definition."

It was like two generations of technology-challenged people trying to have a conversation about stuff we really don't understand at all and trying to fake our way through it.

Dumb and Dumber.

Have things really changed that much? "Brandon, could you get up, find the remote, and change the channel to eight?"

15

Basket of Laundry

The world that we live in is really no different than a basket of laundry. When we wash our laundry, we wash dark colors and light colors, and usually separate them so they will not bleed onto each other or fade to a lighter color. We decide what pieces of clothing are washed in hot water, warm water, and cold water, based on their color or the material they are made of.

Some pieces of clothing are delicate and need a gentle cycle. But some of the colors do fade and cause them to become lighter than they once were. Some of the darker colors may bleed onto the other pieces of clothing and change their color and appearance. When the colors of our laundry change, whether it becomes a lighter, darker, or a mixture of colors, nothing else has changed with our clothes.

The fabric is still the same, the fit is still the same, the size is still the same, the fibers that make up the clothes are still the same.

The only visible change is the color.

Do we judge our clothes differently if our favorite socks are now faded to gray, or our white T-shirt is now a rainbow of a multi-colored designs?

Do we treat our red clothes differently from our green clothes? Do we wear only one color, such as all black or all white, or do we mix and match different colors when we get dressed to create an appearance that is more interesting and fun?

People come in all different colors, shapes, and sizes, too. We have the same organs and in the same places. We all have a heart, lungs, and a brain. We all breathe oxygen. We all bleed when we are cut. We all tan and fade depending on how much sun we expose ourselves to.

We may be a brunette, a blond, or a redhead. We may be tall, short, fat, or thin.

So, you may be asking, *what is the difference between us and our Basket of Laundry?*

We are all the same fabric. We are all made of the same fibers. Our differences, based on what color we are and what we look like, is an illusion.

If one group of people wore only red and another group of people wore only blue, would we treat one group better than the other?

Would the Red group be superior to the Blue group? Who decided this? The Red group ... of course.

What if they remove their shirts and we don't know which color group they belonged to—then what?

How do we decide which group was from the better group, since we only based our judgment on the color of their shirt, and now we don't know which color group they came from?

What if we judged people by their hair color? If they wore a hat—then what? *Our judgment would be blocked.*

What if we judged people by their eye color? If they wore sunglasses—then what? *Our judgment would be blinded.*

Our world is filled with diversity just like a basket of laundry. If we want to have peace on this planet, it will only come with a **Unity of Diversity.** When we finally accept diversity and see people for who they really are, as unique individuals on their own learning path of growth through experience, we will have unity. It is through this acceptance of diversity when we will finally come together in *cooperation instead of competition.* In order for our survival, we all need to come together as one. It is time for all of us to just get along already—to find a new way for PEACE.

PEACE is UNITY. Only then will we be able to come together as one and live in harmony.

We are all made from the same material.

We all need the gentle cycle.

Life is a basket of laundry.

16

Sixteen Candles

There is a reality show on MTV called *My Super Sweet 16*. This is a show where the kids plan, along with their parents, a super extravagant sweet sixteen birthday party for all of their friends at school to attend.

My kids love this show. And like most parents, I end up watching what they watch. It's not a matter of liking the same shows, it's because they hide the TV remote control. I can never seem to change the channel. "But Mom ... we were watching this and we don't know where the remote is!" Yeah right! They usually hide it in the couch pillows!

The extravagant party is held in a hotel ballroom, nightclub, or restaurant that has been rented out for the evening. There is some type of entertainment, usually a very well-known and very expensive band. Most of the time, the headliners are big name performers like Usher and Rihanna.

During the show, the cameras follow the sweet sixteener as they are shopping for party attire, usually with their parents' credit card, and planning their themed party. Showing the teenagers picking out their own birthday present is the highlight of the show. This usually entails a visit to a luxury car dealership where they tell their parents what car they expect to have delivered the night of their birthday party.

The parents spend at least $100,000 or more on the party, including entertainment and the "gift" that is driven away at the end of the big night. The luxury car is presented as the ultimate sweet sixteen gift, and it is brought to the party location. The typical cars have been Mercedes, BMW, Jaguar Hummer, Range Rover, and Lexus. Often these gift cars are nicer than what the parents are driving.

In almost every episode you hear the kids saying, "I get everything I want. If my mom says no, then I go to my dad. One of them always says yes."

And these kids do get what they want. They help plan the party with their parents and pretty much abuse them during the entire party planning process.

The kids whine, "If I don't get the car I want, I will hate you forever!"

"You better get the dress I want—you stupid mom!"

"I'll never talk to you again if Usher doesn't perform at my party! I have to make all of my friends jealous!!!"

"I only turn sixteen once. If I can't have that dress, I won't wear anything! You're ruining my life!!!"

"I only want the Hummer. It better be delivered to my party, and it has to be baby blue!!!"

Yes, this is actual dialogue from the reality show. I sure am glad I don't live in this reality.

In one episode, the birthday girl picked out a $67,000 Lexus convertible for her party gift. "That's a really good price for my happiness," she said to her mom as she was sitting in the car in the dealership showroom. So, her mom has her Lexus convertible delivered to her on her actual birthday instead of presenting the car at her party for all her friends to see and become extremely jealous!

This is tragic, and the sweet girl freaks! "I wanted my car on the day of my party! You ruined everything . . . you stupid, idiotic mom. You ruined my life!!! I didn't want my car now! I hate you! The party is off!"

I don't blame the precious little sweetie. I just can't think of anything worse than having the car of your dreams delivered at the wrong time! "I told you I wanted the car delivered at midnight, and there had to be a full moon! You ruined my life—you stupid dealership! Now I can't have my party!"

Her mom actually gave the car back to the dealership, the birthday girl pulled herself together, and the party was on.

When I watch this show all I want to do is smack the TV. "You little brat. Stop calling your mom a stupid idiot! I am going to smack you right across the television screen."

This is why we need interactive television, to smack around these bratty reality TV stars.

We could have one of those Wii video game systems for these shows. It could have a Wii boxing glove so that we just start hitting these little brats on the screen while they talk. Because it is able to interact with live television, you get to see their heads start to bobble.

This is brilliant! Why hasn't anyone ever thought of this? Am I the only one that likes any of my ideas?

First of all, it is amazing to me that we can now be stars of our own reality. I always knew I was a star. I am starring in my own reality. Where are all the cameras? I have a reality, too!!! Doesn't anyone care about my reality?

Actually, the only reason why I even watch reality TV is because it validates the fact that every other family is just as dysfunctional as mine! When my kids watch *Kate Plus 8*, they always hear me yell, "Mute the television when you watch that show! Kate's yelling and screaming for thirty minutes makes me anxious!"

Reality TV has become a relaxing evening activity. It's a way to bring the family together for bonding and closeness. What family would not want to spend an evening watching *Keeping Up with the Kardashians?* My kids and I enjoy watching the Kardashian sisters bitch-slap each other for thirty minutes. This is how I like to unwind after a stressful day. If I can't bitch-slap those girls myself, at least I get to watch Khloe slap Kim around for awhile.

It's so real! It's just like I am there with them—in the middle of their catfight over clothes, boyfriends, and buying a Bentley. Whenever I see Khloe slap her sisters, I actually duck as a reflex. No wonder it's called reality TV—how clever! Why can't we watch them in 3D?

Do you know what Khloe Kardashian calls a third date? A wedding! Yes, it's true. Khloe is now married. First date—wedding planners. Second date—Vera Wang bridal dress fittings. Third date—Wedding Day!

I really don't blame her. I married someone I knew and it was sooooo boring. It's much more exciting to marry a stranger. You have the rest of your lives to try and get to know each other. Gives you something to do with your life—kinda like a career goal.

"My five-year goal is to get to know my husband a little better. After all, we are officially married!"

Normal people just aren't that entertaining—are we?

These teenagers on *My Super Sweet 16* certainly don't deserve a party; they need boot camp!! Even a boarding school with barbed wire surrounding it would suffice. Why do they call it a sweet sixteen? Are you kidding me! There's nothing sweet about these kids. There have been parties that have been over $400,000 on the show. I'm sure there are some parents still paying off the sweet sixteen party as their kids enter college.

Oprah just doesn't know what a decent birthday party costs these days!

Hey, Oprah, have you seen *My Super Sweet 16*?

I keep tellin' my kids, "Y'know why Oprah is so rich? It's because she doesn't have kids! If I didn't have any kids, I would be that wealthy, too! If I didn't have kids, I would have saved my money and opened up a kids' school in Africa, too." That's what I tell my kids.

"It's because of you two that Africa doesn't have another school. Mommy was going to open one, but then you had another birthday party and bought that new dress!"

Then they have the spinoff reality show called *Exiled*. This show had eight really bratty and spoiled kids from the show *My Super Sweet 16*. These kids had already appeared on *My Super Sweet 16*, had their extravagant parties, and had now reached eighteen years old.

Their parents complained that nothing has changed in the last two years, and their former sweet sixteen is still spoiled and will not accept any responsibility for doing anything around the house. Wow! That's surprising!

So, to help rectify the situation they exile the eight kids to a Third World country for a week to toughen them up and see how others less fortunate live. They live with a family there, work and sleep in tents or huts, eat weird things like roasted guinea pigs, and pick up camel dung with their bare hands!

I think this was a really good family show. I actually enjoyed watching this show with my daughter, who constantly screamed in terror, "Mom, would you ever do that to me?"

"Of course not, honey," I reply. "Just make sure you clean your room by Friday!"

This show is just like the home version of a teenager Scared Straight program. All I have to do during the show is occasionally say, "Hey Morgan, that looks like a nice place. Would you ever like to go there? But honey, it just looks like you may enjoy the culture. Mommy Dearest wasn't implying anything. After the show I would like you to do your laundry and finish your homework, okay sweetie?"

It is so difficult to discipline kids these days, especially teenagers. You can't just sit them in a corner for a time-out anymore. I don't blame these parents for trying to help the kids realize how fortunate they are with their privileged lifestyle by experiencing how people in other cultures live.

I am sure the kids on *Exiled* weren't too traumatized. I have heard that roasted guinea pig tastes like chicken! You can always use the toenail to floss your teeth when you're finished. It makes a nice toothpick!

I know Morgan and Brandon are not going to ask me for a sweet sixteen party. They know I would have the party at IHOP. I always comment on the separate room they have there and how nice it would be to have a party there one day. I think they have a very nice menu. There is something on there for everyone. I like that if I want an omelet for dinner or a patty melt for breakfast, I can order that.

I can bring in my portable boom box that doubles as the car radio inside with me for some nice music to listen to. At the end of the party, I would take all the kids outside to see Brandon's hand-me-down birthday gift: my 2001 Chrysler Minivan.

He would be the envy of all his friends! What other kids get a minibus for their birthday? The other kids have to drive around in those super-cramped, two-seater Mercedes convertibles, and are secretly miserable and wished they had chosen a roomier car.

Actually, I am already planning my kids' sweet sixteens. They are each getting a cake with sixteen candles.

As the girl in the Lexus convertible on *My Super Sweet 16* said . . .

"That's a really good price for my happiness."

17

Prison Break

I was watching the movie *Gridiron* with my son the other night. This is the movie that is based on a true story of young delinquents who ended up in juvenile prison. To prevent the kids from returning to prison and back to gang life once they are released, they decided to help build up these kids' self-esteem and add structure and discipline to their lives. It was decided that football fulfilled this need.

I think this is a great idea! This should be a model for all prisons. Prisoners need more programs to build up self-esteem and help them re-enter society as productive law-abiding citizens. It costs millions of dollars to build a prison and up to one hundred dollars or more a day to house a prisoner.

This is a waste of tax dollars. Why are the people who are not in prison paying for the prisoners? Shouldn't they be paying for their own room and board?

I don't pay for a country club membership I don't use. Why should I pay for a prison I don't use?

Why don't the current residents pay for their own room and board instead of watching television, playing cards, and working out in the prison fitness center. What's next? Bingo night?

Let's give them a job! Did anyone ever think about that? Football is great! Everyone loves watching a good football game, but how many pro teams would want to play the prison teams? Football just wouldn't be the same. "Well, sports fans, we have a special treat for you tonight. The Atlanta Falcons are going to play the Alabama State Prison. The quarterback for Alabama is Randy Brown. Randy has ten years experience in the prison system. He won prisoner of the month in March 2002, and has recently been promoted to kitchen duty."

This is why every prison should have a Drama Club!

The prisoners would not only learn an appreciation for the arts, but would learn how to get along with others, take direction from their peers, and how to talk to large groups of people. The prisoners could learn teamwork in a non-violent way.

Prisoners need more structure to their day. They need a class schedule—a daily agenda! I have a full schedule every day. I don't have time to break the law. (A few traffic tickets don't count!)

Keep them busy. Isn't that what all the parents out there say for the guidelines of good parenting? "Keep 'em busy! Add structure to their life," is the soccer mom cheer!

The prisoners' daily class agenda could look like this: dance class, acting, stage direction, voice lessons, musical theatre, choir, and set design.

Prison Break—the Musical could be the prison version of the very popular *Disney High School Musical*. They could actually go on tour. The ankle chains and handcuffs would not be distracting to the audience. They are playing the role of a prisoner.

There are so many television shows and movies featuring people committing felonies that our prison system could actually be a talent agency for crime dramas and feature films.

There are modeling agencies where they represent models, so how about prison agencies where they represent convicts!

Mug shots . . . head shots . . . all the same thing!

The celebrities who serve jail time could be the guest speakers and teach acting workshops. There's enough of them revolving through the prison. Let's put them to work! I think it's good that these celebrities put their talents to use to serve others when they can, no matter where they are, even if it's the community jail.

By the way, I always wondered why Martha Stewart didn't have her own cooking show from the prison kitchen. Who represented her in that prison agency?!! I would have watched Martha carve that Thanksgiving turkey with the plastic knife!

The acting workshops could train the prisoners to play the most challenging role in Hollywood –themselves.

Did Erin Brockovich play herself? Did Rudy play himself? Absolutely NOT!

It is just too difficult. This requires years of study and training to play yourself. If the prisoners could actually play themselves, this could be worthy of an Oscar. If they need a murderer or a bank robber for the next television show, they can just call the prison agency to get the appropriate convict.

No auditioning would be necessary. Their rap sheet is their resume.

Rap Sheet ... Resume ... all the same thing!

For the prisoners who don't want to act, writing may be a better option. What if there is another writers' strike? We need to be prepared! The prisoners could write from their jail cells.

Just think how realistic our next violent screenplay could be if it was written by a convict who actually committed these crimes. There is nothing like life experience to add realism to your work. This must be why all the violence in the entertainment industry has become so much like real life.

The prisoners must have really paid attention and learned a lot in their acting workshops. What did Robert Downey, Jr. teach them?! They seem to be getting almost every part in Hollywood! The only thing Paris Hilton ever taught during her prison workshop was how to say, "That's Hot! If you want to be my new BFF, you have to say it reeeally sexy!"

Her former cell has never fully recovered from the smell of doo-doo from her seventeen dogs, monkey, ferrets, and her pet goat from their stay during daily visitation hours. The prisoners still miss her traveling circus! If an elephant could have made it through the door of that prison, I'm sure she would have called Africa and ordered one through their mail order catalogue of *African Animals*.

This is why monkeys have now become such a popular family pet. Their new *African Animals* catalogue now accepts online orders!

After all, she once ordered a kangaroo from Australia and had it shipped to her house, only to send it back after a friend told her it would grow really really big and start punching her. All I can say about that is—"That's Hot!"

Well, Robert Downey, Jr. taught the prisoners a little too well during his prison jaunts. These convicts are working sixteen-hour days with all the parts they are constantly offered. Mostly leading roles, too! The prison agency has been swamped with day and night phone calls requesting murderers, bank robbers, serial killers, and a bunch of psycho people for random smaller parts.

They just can't seem to keep up with the demand for all the violent television shows and movies! They don't have the personnel of the larger talent agencies that are not afforded the twenty-four-hour security and surveillance of the prison system.

Against their better judgment, the prison agency decided to go ahead and hire an inmate to help out with answering the phone, but the next day the phone was gone. Apparently, the cord seemed to be a valuable asset.

Hey Hollywood! The prisoners and their agents have been working overtime with all of the violence on television and the movie screens. Let's give them some time off.

Maybe we should try a less violent vocation for when it's time for the inmates to finally come back to work.

Instead of a Drama Club, we could try a Cooking Club.

I hear Martha is cooking a Thanksgiving turkey again this year, and she's carving it with a real knife! Let's let the prisoners watch her show. Prisoners like pumpkin gnocchi, too!

The prisoners could cook along with Martha step-by-step. They could have a prison camera to video the inmates cooking along with Martha making her own gourmet recipes. Martha could greet her new colleagues during the show. The camera could switch footage of the Martha Stewart kitchen and the prison kitchen. Her show would be a lot more interesting and exciting!

Watching the inmate food fights and the plastic cutlery melting while cooking the hot dishes would make for great reality television. It can be difficult to stir boiling spaghetti with a plastic spoon. The viewers would have empathy for the prison chefs and call in to offer advice for cooking with limited utensils.

The *Martha Stewart Show* could start off like this: "Hello inmates and former friends. Also, a shout out to my loyal viewers at home who didn't mind my brief hiatus during my weight loss program at the federal prison in West Virginia.

"I lost twenty pounds in five months during the popular new prison diet for celebrities. I got a chance to make some new girlfriends, eat the healthy prison food, work out every night in the recreation center (except for the evenings the women reserved the room for orgies), and teach yoga classes.

"The security guards were just like our own private personal trainers. The guards made sure we stayed at the prison weight loss center until we reached our weight loss goal, which incidentally coincided with the completion of our prison term.

"After five months on my prison diet, I feel better than ever, and I am ready to cook!

"Today, we are making a new recipe that received five stars in our test kitchen. The recipe was sent in from a viewer in Atlanta, Georgia. She said it's her kids' favorite and they gobble it up every time. It's a meatloaf with a chocolate glaze. For dessert, we will have fresh strawberries dipped in the leftover chocolate. Thank you, Melissa Mintz, for sending this recipe to us.

"I know it will be delicious! Chop! Chop! Everyone at home and my prison friends–let's get started!"

The prisoners are always complaining about the food. If we let them watch the cooking shows, they can rotate through the prison kitchen and learn how to make their own gourmet dishes. Many of them have already met Martha during the meet and greet for all new inmates. It would be just like cooking with an old friend, Martha in her brightly lit and designer decorated television kitchen and the inmates in the prison kitchen.

Everyone could pitch in and work together. The inmates could be rehabilitated through cooking! *Cooperation through Cuisine* could be the next hit prison reality TV show!

World-renowned chef Gordon Ramsay from *Hell's Kitchen* has volunteered to prepare the prisoners for their new reality show by hosting a week-long cooking boot camp. *Hell's Kitchen* is a reality cooking show where aspiring young chefs compete for a chance to win the executive chef position at one of Gordon Ramsay's restaurants.

If anyone can get these prisoners in cooking shape, it's Gordon Ramsey. He can take a cook with little experience and turn them into an expert chef in no time. Chef Ramsay is perfect for the job. With his motivational style and encouraging comments—like "Move your ass, you fat cow! You're crap! Are you a dumb blonde? It tastes like gnat piss! You donkey!"—it will surely inspire the novice prison cooks.

By the way, where does Gordon Ramsay go to drink gnat piss? Is it served in a tall frothy glass on draft at the traditional London pub?

Many people may consider Chef's Ramsay's style as verbally abusive, but he is really very passionate about his cooking, and he's British. Maybe that's how they talk in England at their local restaurants. If I went out for fish and chips in London and asked my waiter for tartar sauce, maybe he would say, "Piss off, you fat cow! Move your ass and get it yourself!!!"

We probably shouldn't be so judgmental. After all, every culture has their own unique customs! My personal favorite comment from Chef Ramsay to his cooks: "You're sweating in the food!!! Look at what you're doing! The food's too salty!"

I think that's good advice, no matter what career path you end up choosing. I will definitely teach this lesson to my children. I wouldn't want them to grow up to be the kind of adults that sweat profusely into their food!

If I want my food seasoned, I usually prefer table salt over globs of drippy face sweat pouring into it. If I didn't order face sweat dripping from the chin and nose from the menu, I think it should not appear in my meal.

Watching this on the show is really gross. For me, it's even grosser than all the chefs' fingertips that have been accidently cut off from slicing up the vegetables. This leaky faucet-style drippy face sweat is like watching someone work out on the treadmill for an hour and capturing their sweat in a cup, and then pouring it on top of your food. It must be like 110 degrees in that kitchen. Maybe they really are trying to recreate hell.

He dismisses the contestants at the end of the show after the completion of the dinner service saying, "Piss off! Get some sleep!" With his British accent it sounds almost endearing.

On every season there is always an appetizer of risotto. I never realized how difficult risotto is to cook. But it must be, because on every season you hear him screaming, "Where's the risotto? Where's the risotto? The risotto needs to be seasoned! It's too bland! It's too mushy!" One of the highest compliments from Chef Ramsay a contestant can get on this show is: "Very nice, that risotto."

Risotto-obsessed Chef Ramsay will have those prison cooks promptly ready for prime-time cooking. The inmates will be too busy with their cooking reality show to appear in any more violent crime dramas. "Tell my agent I can't appear on *CSI*. I'm in charge of cooking the risotto tonight!"

Eventually, due to a lack of talent to play all of the homicidal roles, the violence in our entertainment will be replaced with more genteel family-style programs. Finally, we have a new hit TV show to replace the popular crime drama *Prison Break.*

That show was always so predictable anyhow. Every show is the same theme—someone is going to do something violent and break the law! We know how it is going to end—they will be in prison … Duh!

Cooperation through Cuisine will not be a predictable show at all! We won't know how the pumpkin gnocchi is going to come out until the end of the show! That's when the camera does a close up of their smiling face as the convicts are sampling the finished pasta.

And besides, it's about time we have some tough chefs in the kitchen. Somebody has to finally stand up to Chef Gordon Ramsay and tell him to "piss off!"

18

Homeowners' Association (HA)

Have you ever wondered what happened to the tattletale from elementary school, the kid who always had to tell the teacher everything everyone was doing so that no one could ever get away with anything against the rules that the teacher made up? These rules were constantly changing and no one seemed to know what the set of rules really were. They just knew that they were in trouble if these unwritten and ever-changing rules weren't followed.

Well, I know what happened to that kid.

Little Jimmy grew up, got married, bought a house in the burbs, and now has a prominent position in his neighborhood.

Finally, a position of prestige where his talents, which have been honed since childhood, have been put to good use. Little Jimmy, the former classroom spy who found a position of power as the classroom tattletale and teacher's pet mole, has now become a member of our very own Homeowners' Association.

Yes, it's true! Little Jimmy is now James, the Homeowners' Violations Patrolman.

James travels through your neighborhood in his unmarked patrol car to check and see if any homeowners have violated the rules.

What rules? Who really knows what these guidelines are? But, not to worry … James seems to know what the rules are, and if he decides we have broken any of them, we will be notified by a nasty letter from our Homeowners' Association.

This letter usually includes the name of the violation, then a threat of a fine in a certain dollar amount if this violation continues. If you receive several violations, there is a clause in the letter which threatens to put a lien on your home if you do not make the required changes. I have received several violations from James, the patrolman, for various neighborhood crimes.

I received a letter for having a *couple of small weeds* in my pine straw island near my rose bushes. I do have a crew of professional landscapers who come every two weeks to take care of all the lawn requirements, but a fast growing weed must have popped its head through the dirt a little too quickly.

Those nasty little convicts! No wonder why we put them on death row with weed killer.

I also received a violation for my mailbox leaning a little off-center. This is the neighborhood approved mailbox that, of course, matches all of the other neighborhood approved mailboxes in the subdivision.

This infraction must have been unsightly for the entire neighborhood. So, I would like to take this opportunity to apologize to everyone out there about how my unsightly mailbox must have offended you, your children, and your pets, who weren't able to pee around it appropriately. As soon as I received the letter, I rectified this situation immediately by giving the mailbox a little tap with my hand to move it two inches to the right.

We can send a man to the moon, but we don't have the technology to prevent a mailbox from ever leaning. Why is this not a potential college major for our young students for their course of study? Obviously, there is a need for this unmet technology!

I also received a letter from the *Homeowners' Association* after my entire front and side yard were TP'ed (toilet papered) by a neighborhood kid. The letter stated that the way I decorated my yard was an embarrassment to the neighborhood and should be rectified immediately or a severe fine would be imposed.

All I can say about that is, "James . . . GROW UP AND GET A REAL JOB!!!"

Now, you know why our neighborhoods are governed by the Homeowners' Association (HA). The first letter they send is HA—the next letter they send to you is HA-HA and the third letter is . . .

HA-HA-HA

19

Naked Neighbors

Well, now that school is out and it is summer, my kids want to go to the neighborhood pool as much as possible. Why shouldn't they? We pay for the use of the neighborhood pool through our Homeowners' Association.

I had already paid my fines for my mailbox leaning a little off-center and for the two wicked weeds that popped up in my pine straw island, so we were awarded our annual neighborhood pool key.

School is out. The sun is shining. It's time to put on the swimsuit and swim with the neighbors. When I was a kid, we didn't have the neighborhood pool. We had a lawn sprinkler. The sprinkler was the neighborhood pool.

If you turned on the sprinkler, the neighborhood kids came—invited or not. The coolest sprinkler was the one that went back and forth, and you took turns running through it. When you got thirsty, you just opened your mouth and took a big gulp of water. Nowadays, it would be appalling to drink from your hose, especially since most people don't even drink tap water.

"Oh my gosh! My dear little Michael drank from your sprinkler! Was it filtered?" This would be the reaction today of parents whose kids have choices of spring water, distilled water, electrolyte water, flavored water, and purified water. I go to the grocery store and stand in the water section for ten minutes trying to figure out all the waters. I'm not even sure what the difference is.

Since it is now a Homeowners' Association faux pas to swim in your lawn sprinkler, we opt for the neighborhood pool. It just seems so weird to lie on a lounger in your swimsuit with all the other neighbors. You feel like you're all just hangin' out in your underwear swimming in the water.

The rest of the year, you are all fully clothed and then suddenly the pool is open, and it's time to get naked. I have rarely seen my neighbors in any type of body-flattering clothing. I can't remember the last time I saw a woman in the neighborhood wearing a tube top or sports bra, exposing her tummy, or showing any cleavage at all.

All of a sudden, at the pool, these are the women who wear the skimpiest and most revealing swimsuits. Same thing with the men. I have only seen the men in long shorts and T-shirts. Rarely do any of the men even wear a tank top or shorts above the knee.

So now, these guys are shirtless and wearing little short-style swimsuits and some have even ventured to the man bikini. The strange thing is that if you saw your neighbor mowing his yard in his little mankini, you would stare and think he has lost his mind! If you see him and there is any water around—even a small inflatable pool in his yard—you would not think this attire is inappropriate at all.

This just seems odd to me. Any type of immodest dress is appropriate if there is water around.

Even when we are at the water parks, I always comment to the kids when we stand in the maze of a line for thirty minutes to ride the water. "Doesn't it seem strange! We all just stand around in our lycra underwear and check each other out!"

I always thought it was bizarre that when I am at a company meeting, if I had on a swimsuit while we were having drinks at the hotel bar, I would probably be fired, or at least reprimanded for dressing indecently and unprofessionally. If we move our party to the outside bar by the pool and I wore a swimsuit, nobody would think that was inappropriate at all.

It's like ... hey, there's a small body of water in close proximity. It's not important if any of us can actually see the pool; it's a silent understanding that we all share. There's water around—lycra underwear is now appropriate. You can strip down and have a glass of wine with your boss. It doesn't matter if the only pool on the property is a four-person Jacuzzi over yonder—it's still water!

I realize I probably spend way too much time thinking about these things, but come on—isn't this weird?

Most parents would not take their kids to see an R-rated movie with nudity, and yet they will let their kids go to the neighborhood pool! I have seen more nudity at the neighborhood pool. Anything seems to go, including thong bikinis. There's always some lady swimming in her thong bikini. It just doesn't seem right to see your neighbor's butt at the pool, especially while they are swimming laps!

There's nothing you can do about it. It is the Homeowners' Golden Rule. We can pick our homes, but we can't pick our neighbors!

You know what makes me happy? A *FOR SALE* sign. This justifies a champagne toast with close friends and family. That's what I am saving my bottle of Veuve Clicquot for! A For Sale sign is actually an opportunity. This is another opportunity to swap our neighbors and hope for an upgrade. *A sale of a house is like being at the craps table in Vegas. The odds aren't great, but at least you have a chance at winning.*

It's a ray of hope that the new neighbors are going to be less irritating, annoying, and psycho than the previous ones. This is why I think we should have a neighborhood catalogue with pool uniforms that would be appropriate to wear at the neighborhood pool.

I wouldn't walk around my neighbors' kids in a skimpy bra and panties, but now I can wear the same thing—in spandex—at the pool. The catalogue could contain a choice of three styles for women: a two-piece swimsuit in either a modest bikini or a tankini style; and, of course, the one piece suit to keep the tummy flab from hangin' out. There could be a couple of shorts styles for the men.

We could have our neighborhood logo printed on them and be part of the newly formed Neighborhood Pool Club, with pool parties and cookouts! What a selling feature for potential home buyers in the 'hood. We are a family-oriented neighborhood with great values. We even have neighborhood pool uniforms to protect your little children from swimming with a naked butt in their face as they are diving for their pool toy.

Our neighborhood pool has been closed several times during the summer because of poop or vomit in the water. A few accidents have occurred where a baby's swim diaper came off or the poopie escaped from the diaper. It looked like someone threw some Tootsie Rolls in there as a dive toy.

I happened to be at the pool one day and a kid was playing and swallowed too much water, then started vomiting in the pool. We were all evacuated, and the pool was closed for several days. You would think there was some type of nuclear accident. We were herded out very quickly and we weren't allowed anywhere near the pool for days.

There is also a small baby pool adjacent to the big pool so the little babies can sit and play with their water toys. You can always spot the baby pool: the water is always a light yellow. Have you ever wondered why the baby pool is so warm?

When my kids were little, I never allowed them to swim in the pee pool. I always played with them in the big pool. I would put them in their inflatable floating pool toys and give them rides through the pool.

These are just a few of the things you can actually see in the pool. How many times have you seen people spit out water or blow their nose in the pool? People have farted in the pool, too! You just can't see it.

Most families bring food to the pool for their kids to munch on so they can enjoy hours of play without having to go home for snacks and lunch. There is usually food floating around in the water, especially near the steps where you enter and exit the pool. The steps seem to be a wonderful place to dine where you can enjoy Cheetos, chips, pizza, and cookies while staying cool in the water.

I always wondered why they don't just throw the picnic table in the shallow end of the pool!!!

It would be just like those resort hotels where they have the swim-up bar to enjoy a tropical cocktail or soda to quench your thirst on a sultry day. We could have a swim-up snack bar in our very own neighborhood pool.

We could even rope off the picnic area of the pool just like they have a rope to separate the deep end. It would be easy to clean the tables—just use the pool water. The lifeguard could also play host/hostess and seat their pool guests. It gets a little boring for them to just sit in a chair, tan, and listen to their favorite radio station for hours and hours.

We would be the envy of all the other neighborhoods: pool uniforms and a swim-up snack bar. We'll never have to take another summer vacation again! I'll just bring my inflatable palm tree and put it by my lounger, and it'll be just like being in Florida. The kids will love it!

Wait till I tell them Mom's brilliant idea of vacationing at the neighborhood pool with the neighbors! Maybe we'll even throw some sand in the pool to get the beach effect!

My sister and I actually live in the same neighborhood. She decided to build a pool in her backyard to enjoy her own private pool with her family. When she built the pool a neighbor said to her, "What's the matter, Michele, you don't like the neighborhood pool?" Well ... duh!

There's something to be said for being able to enjoy a nice swim without diluted vomit, spit, snot, pee, pizza, and floating turds.

It's also kinda nice to wear whatever swimsuit you want at your pool, or wear none at all.

Well, summer is coming to end. I thought I looked pretty good at the pool swimming in my thong bikini!

I got a nice tan. Swapped recipes at the swim-up snack bar, and swam with the inflatable dolphins in the deep end!

WHAT A GREAT VACATION!!!

See ya next summer!

20

Handicap Parking

My kids always yell at me for trying to park in the handicap parking spaces, but I just tell them, "Shut up, kids. They have wheels—they can ride in. I'm the one that has to walk!" What's the difference when they are closer to the door to ride in and then roll around the store for three hours?

I see them at the mall passing me every time. I'm still at Auntie Anne's Pretzels, and they're flying past me already at the Gap. When I see someone get out of the car in the handicap parking space and walk into the mall, I just know I am not the only one to glance over to try and figure out what their disability is. Well, they are walking—no crutches, no bandages anywhere. What the heck is wrong with them? How did they get that handicap parking tag?!

You see them walking to the door and you start to move ahead of them. You're thinking, *I'm not gonna let a handicap person get to the door before me.* Then it becomes a race. You're supposed to be handicap. You took the space by the entrance, now get behind me! *Hey buddy, your moving way too fast to get that prime parking space!*

Handicap parking has become a lifetime free pass for great parking and avoiding long lines. You can use it to get the best parking spaces and you can use it to get to the front of the line at all the theme parks. Just wear it on a string around your neck and you get to move to the front of the line for Space Mountain at Disney World.

It doesn't matter if you're running to the line; you've got a handicap parking tag around your neck! They can't prove you don't have a disability! Make 'em prove it! You don't have to show your medical records to have a handicap pass. Actually, you don't need to show any ID at all.

It doesn't matter if your grandmother died, and that's all she left you! You now have a lifetime pass for front row parking!

In Florida, when you establish residency, they must automatically give you a handicap parking pass. I know when my mom moved to Florida, she got one. All of her friends have one as well. I asked, "Mom, how did you get that disability card for your car? You get front row parking, but then you walk for at least two miles in the mall!"

They must figure if you don't need it now, eventually you will. Hang on to it, or lease it to your friends on a lease purchase plan!

Why don't you have to show ID when you use a handicap parking pass? Why are these passes transferable?! Not going to the mall today? Can I borrow your pass? My mom used to borrow her friend's card before she got her own. Now she rents hers out! I said, "Mom, what are you doing? You need to charge for that! You should establish a price list by the 'hour' and for the 'day' to use your handicap pass for great parking!

"These malls are packed," I continued, still trying to convince her of this great business opportunity. "All the snowbirds are coming in for the winter, and they will be competing for the good spaces! God forbid anyone has to actually walk into the mall," I said in a slightly sarcastic tone.

Nowadays, you can get a front row parking pass even without the blue card to hang in your window. Many parking lots now have these strange reserved spaces near the entrance. They have signs on a pole in front of the parking spaces to let you know who can park there.

It's the new specialty parking—customers with children, expectant mothers, senior citizens, woman with infant, etc. How are these businesses getting away with this?

This is discrimination. What's next? Are *all* the front spaces for our shopping centers, restaurants, and other businesses going to have reserved spaces? Are the parking lots going to keep adding more signs for parking: men with heart trouble;

women with yeast infections; cancer survivors; Botox babes; diabetics; bipolar disorder; women with breast implants; men with prostate trouble; customers with hemorrhoids. . . .

Healthy people are actually discriminated against. We get the worst parking! They will have open parking for the healthy people in the back of the parking lot a few miles away from the front door. I will be in the back parking lot with all the other healthy people waiting for the shuttle bus to transport me to the front entrance!

I didn't know when I was pregnant that it was considered a disability and would have qualified me for a front row parking space! Why was I walking through a parking lot?

Apparently, now that I am a woman with child it qualifies me into the elite parking club as well. I don't even understand these parking signs. There is no age limit on there for children. What if my children are now adults— can I still park there? Do the kids have to be with me? What if they live out of town?

I usually park in those reserved spaces because I think it is ridiculous to have them! I have parked in the pregnant woman's space several times. They can't prove I'm not pregnant! Is there going to be a parking lot monitor to request that I show a pregnancy test?

I'm just waiting for someone to ask me to pee in a cup before I park!

For the record, pregnant women need to walk. They need the exercise! It's good for them. I walked when I was pregnant.

So what? They are thirty feet closer to the door so they can walk inside the shopping center for three hours!

The only place that it would be helpful to have a pregnant woman parking space is at every fast-food restaurant to make sure there is a space near the door so that women can run in and pee.

Sometimes, one space can make all the difference of how you smell the rest of the day!

To make matters worse, these specialty spaces are all on the honor system.

I was at BJ's Membership Club today, and there was a parking space reserved for customer with infant. The store was especially crowded, and I saw that parking space open. I drove past the space and decided I will do the honorable thing today and let a customer with an infant take the space, since it was a little chilly outside.

I thought it would be a nice gesture to allow a parent to be a little closer to the door to get the cute little newborn out of the cold. I looked in my rearview mirror, and the lady in the car behind me pulled into the space without hesitation. I watched her get out of the car, without an infant, and rush into the store hoping not to be seen.

"Darn . . . I let that space go!" I muttered to myself.

The senior citizen parking spaces are popping up in parking lots as well. I have yet to see a senior citizen get out of a car in this reserved space. What if we see a seventy-five-year-old woman get out of a car in this space and she has had a face lift and looks forty, or if we see a man that is thirty, but prematurely gray and looks sixty-five. How can anyone monitor this?

Why are these spaces being reserved anyway!? These are not disabilities! Americans need more exercise. What's next? Will we have a moving sidewalk like they have at the airports installed from the parking lot to the front entrance?

Why don't we just put a hot dog stand along the way so we can have a snack while we are exerting ourselves riding the sidewalk?

I certainly do think that there are times when a person with a disability should not be walking around in a parking lot. It can be very dangerous. There are no rules and regulations in a parking lot. A parking lot is considered private property! This is why cars can cut through wherever they want.

We have cars going up and down the aisles while other cars are cutting across the parking lot. Some drivers are driving making horizontal lines, other drivers are driving in vertical lines. A parking lot is a free-for-all! Wherever there is an open space, people will drive.

This is why I think all short people should have a handicap parking pass. If you are under five feet tall, you should be able to qualify for handicap parking! I can barely see you out of the back window of my minivan when I back up. When minivans, trucks, and sport utility vehicles back out of the parking spaces, we can't see "little people" or people in wheelchairs!

It amazes me that there is no designated pedestrian walkway to your car. Cars are driving in any open space in all directions, backing out of the spaces as there are people behind them walking in or walking out of the stores.

The drivers are talking on their cell phones with their car radios blaring! If you scream while they are backing out and running over your foot, they can't hear you! They have a rock concert going on in their vehicles with surround sound!

They have one hand on the steering wheel and another hand on the Starbucks coffee cup, with a sandwich on their lap that they are trying to eat by alternating the hand on the steering wheel with picking up the sandwich and cramming it into their mouth.

I am surprised there aren't more accidents with people getting hit by a car in the parking lots. Just the other day, I was walking into Target with Morgan, and a lady was backing out of her space and didn't even bother to look behind her. "Morgan! Watch out!!!" I screamed frantically! The lady rolled her window down, smiled at us, said a quick, "Sorry," and sped off.

If I was walking up and down a busy street on the main road, dodging in and out of traffic, walking down the middle of the road, I would be stopped by police and be given a ticket or thrown in jail. I can do this all day in any parking lot!

Kids these days are too sedentary and spend way too much time playing video games. They need to get out and exercise! Why aren't the elementary schools taking their kids out into the busy school parking lots for exercise during the required gym class.

Kids are tired of playing dodge ball. They need a new game—dodge the cars.

Kids already know the rules of play. They have played this game a million times while out with their parents. Run around for an hour and try not to get hit by the moving cars. It's much more challenging, and the last kid standing is the winner!

Why are there no designated pedestrian walkways around the busy retail stores and mall parking lots? The pedestrians are all walking aimlessly through the parking lots; nobody can remember where they parked their cars anymore! The parking lots keep getting bigger and bigger.

I never remember where I park my car. Not only can I not remember where I parked, but I can't remember which car I drove! Most families have more than one car these days. It's so embarrassing! When the grocery baggers walk me out to the car to assist me, I take them on a grand tour!

I have reminded the employees how fortunate they are that when they help me out to my car, they get a guaranteed ten-minute parking lot break. "Isn't it a beautiful day for a walk? Let's go down this aisle again. I know it's around here somewhere! Did you happen to see what car I pulled up in?!"

I finally found my car located way in the back of the dull gray, concrete parking lot. I didn't remember having such a long walk when I entered the store. No wonder I am so confused; all the parking spaces look alike. Why aren't they color-coded? If I parked in the pretty purple space, I think I would remember!

I decided to head off to the mall to continue my shopping. After a full day of exhausting shopping, I realized it was getting late. *Time for me to get home to the kids*, I thought, as I daydreamed about what to make them for dinner that evening with the groceries I'd purchased earlier in the day.

As I walked through the crowded mall parking lot, I heard a woman's voice yell to me. "Excuse me, ma'am. Did you happen to see my car? I am parked in the reserved space for splinter in foot!"

"I saw it, lady," I hurriedly replied. "It's in the second row in the foot section by the ingrown toenail space."

With my arms full of shopping bags, I finally made it to the shuttle stop at the same time the little bus pulled up.

"Hey driver, can you take me to my car? I parked in space number two thousand and twelve."

21

Trick-or-Treat

I always enjoy celebrating holidays. I usually associate holidays with getting time off work. When my company sends out the holiday calendar for the upcoming year, the first thing I do is take out my calendar and mark all the holidays for the year so I have something to look forward to.

The majority of holidays are associated with time off work, with the exception of Valentine's Day and Halloween. I have always thought of Halloween as a very strange holiday. I think for most kids it is their second favorite holiday, trailing right behind Christmas.

I know when I was a kid I looked forward to Halloween all year. Free candy! This is an incredible concept for a kid to understand, because all the other days throughout the year parents constantly yell at them: "NO CANDY!"

How did this holiday come about where one day every year it is considered a social expectation to give all the neighborhood kids who come to your door free candy?

This holiday actually started centuries ago in England and Ireland. The poor citizens in a community would go door to door begging for treats in exchange for a promise of saying a prayer for the dead. This is why people still occasionally refer to trick-or-treating as going out begging. The treats were cakes or pastries referred to as soul cakes. This tradition was called going a-souling.

In the early days, people would dress up to resemble the dead spirits they were saying a prayer for, like ghosts, witches, and skeletons. This has evolved to our modern-day trick-or-treat. Instead of baking pastries and cakes, we go to the store and stock up on big bags of candy to give out to a hundred or more kids.

This holiday has become so important to the kids that parents try to take off from work early to beat the rush and get their kids fed and dressed to go out and beg for candy. There is certainly no time to cook dinner when you're looking for batteries for the bloody chain saws and talking vampire heads. Halloween has become one of the busiest pizza delivery nights, trailing slightly behind Super Bowl Sunday.

Halloween is the Super Bowl for the candy companies. This is their chance to compete to see who can make the grossest and scariest looking candy.

The packaging of the candy has changed and is now in the orange Halloween wrappers. The chocolate is shaped like pumpkins, ghosts, and witches. The gummy candy now resembles all kinds of disgusting things that make you cringe just looking at it: bloody eyeballs and bloody amputated body parts. You can buy hard candy that is packaged in the shape of assorted bones for those who prefer something a little more crunchy.

Every year I buy candy twice. I initially buy candy a couple of weeks before Halloween during the pre-holiday sales. Most stores offer discounts to start moving the surplus bags of candy off their shelves with incentives such as, buy one bag—get one free.

My subconscious mind apparently hears: save one bag—eat one bag. My candy bar stash, originally hidden from my kids who constantly say, "When are we going to buy the candy? I want to pick it out," starts to dwindle to a supply for about twenty kids. So, I rush out the night before Halloween with the kids in tow, hoping to hit a mad dash for candy sale.

"See ... I told you I would take you to pick out the candy. You each get to pick out one bag," I tell them as I encourage them toward the Snickers, Butterfingers, and Twix bars, and away from the Starburst, gummy bears and Tootsie Pops. *If I am going to buy candy, I might as well buy what I like!* I silently rationalize—someone has to eat the leftovers.

The kids start trick-or-treating as soon as dusk settles on October 31st, the eve of free candy. This means that if I don't give candy to whoever comes to my door, I may be in store for a trick.

Who knows what the trick could be. It could be my yard being toilet papered or my car being vandalized. When I was a kid, the homes that had their lights off and did not give out candy usually got their windows "soaped" by the older kids. The kids would carry a bar of soap with them and draw designs on the windows. Every year I would hear parents complain how difficult it was to get the soap off their windows.

Nowadays if the lights are on in your house or front porch, you are considered open for business. The kids know you are home and ready to pass out candy.

There is a lot of preparation to get ready for Halloween: buying the candy; picking out the kids' costumes; and decorating the yard so it will look scary for the little beggars.

The front yards are decorated with: talking skulls; flying ghosts; realistic-looking fake spiders; bloody figurines like Frankenstein with a removable electronic head; amputated body parts with lots of fake blood; and skeletons on the ground in front of a tombstone.

It's amazing to me that we even let these little kids out of the house!

Most parents would not allow their children to see a scary horror movie because they don't want their kids exposed to blood and gore. However, on Halloween night we let them dress up like scary dead people and run around the neighborhood with battery-operated chain saws and bloody rubber knives.

"It's all in fun," the parents tell their little kids as they start to cry. "That huge hairy spider on the door isn't real. Do you want to touch it, Susie? Let's take a picture of you and Mommy by the bloody head."

No wonder kids today are so messed up! We scrutinize the television shows they watch to make sure they are not violent. Most parents would not take their kids to see a movie replete with blood and gore. On Halloween, they'll dress the kid up as a scary vampire and smear fake blood all over his face.

"Austin, you're going to get a lot of candy with that costume! Let Mommy take some pictures for your grandparents!"

All year long we tell kids they can't have candy. Then Halloween comes, and we strategize with them so they can get as much candy as possible.

"Susie! Mommy told you not to wear the Cinderella slippers! If you had your sneakers on you would be at the Mintz's house by now. Run Susie . . . Run!!!"

It is such a drag when I take my kids to the house on the hill, and we finally reach the front door only to be greeted with some crappy candy. How about a social expectation that if your house is on a hill that rivals the beginner hill on Vail mountain, you'd better be giving out some really good candy!

"Are you kiddin' me? One teeny weenie Tootsie Roll? These things come in like a thousand to a bag. The kids get ONE Tootsie Roll?!" If you are not going to sit in a chair at the bottom of the hill and give out candy to save the kids a hike, at least give out good candy!!

Kids remember this stuff, too! They remember the house that gave out the good stuff. The big candy bars, the Swedish fish, the bloody eyeball gummies. . . . These are the homes they target early in the night before the candy runs out, and the lights are turned off.

I actually don't mind giving out the candy. I enjoy eating some of the candy in between the visits. I think it's kinda cute when the kids compliment me on my candy selection. "Wow, Ms. Mintz, I really like the 100 GRAND Bars. I haven't gotten one of those yet!"

These kids are really smart and network with each other. Most of them already know what candy you are giving out before they come to your door. "My friend Austin said you were giving these out. They're my favorite!"

This is all part of their strategy to get as much candy as quickly as possible. If you are giving out tapioca pudding cups, homemade cookies, toothbrushes, or the loose spare pennies from the bottom of your purse, you can rest assured you will have a quiet evening.

I have to admit, some of the costumes are really cute, especially the little kids who are pre-school age and younger. The girls are usually wearing Barbie or one of the Disney characters like Cinderella or Snow White. The boys usually go for more of the superhero costumes like Batman, Superman, or Spiderman.

The grade school kids either go for the career category like football players, policemen, firemen, doctors, and nurses, or they wear the really gory skeleton costumes with the scary masks.

I took Morgan to a local party supply store to buy a Halloween costume for trick-or-treat this year. At the store, there is a wall adorned with pictures of the available costumes. Each costume has a name and a corresponding number.

This store is all set for a large crowd of trick-or-treaters and partygoers to purchase their holiday wear, and they have ramped up with additional personnel. The back of the store resembles an FBI covert operation stakeout. The employees, walking around with their microphone and earpiece headgear, constantly talk back and forth in a series of codes.

The employees working the floor yell a series of numbers into their microphone; a few minutes later, several workers come out from the back storage room and call out the numbers corresponding to the costume for the awaiting customer. As the customers all run toward the employee holding up the costume, the entire scene starts to resemble a rugby match with a missed tackle.

"What costume do you like, Mommy?" Morgan asks.

I can hardly reply. I'm too dumbfounded looking at the pictures of the costumes on the wall. All I think is, *When did the costumes start looking ... so ... skanky? I don't remember the costumes looking so slutty in previous years.*

The majority of the costumes for the pre-teen girls are so revealing. It did not matter what the costume was. It could be a referee or a lady bug. The standard is a super-short mini-skirt and a revealing low-cut top.

Some of the costumes have garter straps that attach to the thigh-high black boot tops or stockings. The pictures of the costumes on the wall show the girls wearing either knee-high, platform disco boots or spiked high heels.

If it weren't for all the Halloween paraphernalia in the store, I would think I was in a clothing boutique for exotic dancers looking for a new outfit that would assure them big tips for the night.

Even sweet little Dorothy from the *Wizard of Oz* looks like a Halloween hussy with her little mini, checkered blue and white dress just barely covering her upper thighs. It seems that *Halloween Ho* is the new trick-or-treat attire for young girls and adult women.

"I don't know, Morgan. What are you thinking about trying on?" I finally answer, trying not to sound too freaked out and uncool.

"I think I like the witch costume. Can you tell them I want to try it on? I'll go ahead and wait in the line for the dressing room."

Morgan tries on the witch costume and opens up the dressing room door so I can have a look.

"Well . . . do you like it?" she asks a little tentatively, hoping for my approval.

Morgan stands there in the shortest skirt I have ever seen her wear with a little black corset over a ruffled white off-the-shoulder top.

"Morgan ... You're going to wear a zip-up sweatshirt over that top," I yell so fast I could hardly even understand what I'd just said. "I have a white one—it'll match fine! It's going to be cold, so you'll need to cover up."

I barely even take a breath before I continue, "You can wear your white leggings under that skirt. It's ... soooo ... short on you. I want you to wear your tennis shoes, okay? No heels!"

Did I miss something? I thought to myself as she was changing out of the costume. I don't remember the costumes being so revealing in the past for young girls.

In truth, the only thing I really liked about the outfit was the bright, orange and white knee-high socks and the tall, pointed, candy corn striped witch hat.

While she was in the dressing room changing, I had images of her trick-or-treating with her friends in their slutty Halloween costumes.

I started cringing as I imagined the neighbors asking ...

"So Morgan, what are you dressed up as?"

"I'm a skanky witch. Can I have a Reese's?"

How did these costumes evolve into a burlesque show? When I was a kid, a witch costume, like most of the costumes, usually came with a long cape and a mask. The costumes weren't sexy at all! They weren't even form fitting. With the mask on you couldn't tell if it was a girl or boy beggar.

Back in the day, no one really cared if they looked sexy while running in the dark from one house to another. The goal was to get candy and get a lot of candy before the porch light was turned off.

Evidently, now Halloween is more of a Mardi Gras without the beads. The girls are expected to be scantily clad while running to each house in platform knee-high stripper boots or four-inch stilettos while lugging a pillow case full of assorted candy.

What will next year be like? Halloween harlots dressed in wicked and scary lingerie?

Will we hear Eric talk on his headgear to Joey in the stock room: "A customer out here wants to try on number two hundred and thirty-seven. It's the pumpkin thong and the matching orange garter belt with the black fishnet stockings. Hey, Joey, don't forget the matching top. It's the one with the little black string and two small pumpkins on the front."

Now I know why women sew. It may be a good time to learn. There's something to be said for Mom making your floor-length oversized costume.

The teenage boys seem to have opted for a come as you are costume. As soon as you open the door they have their hand out and just say, "Hey!" They take the candy, stuff it in their mouth, and throw the wrapper on your front lawn.

There is no age limit for the trick-or-treaters. I think that if these kids are already shaving, they are too old to be out trick-or-treating!

I said to my son, "Hey, Brandon, a 'kid' just came to my door for trick-or-treat. He had a full beard and a moustache. Don't you think he is a little too old for this?"

Of course, I am going to give him candy. My car is parked in the driveway. Do I want my car vandalized because I didn't give the kid his candy?

I realize I did not go to law school, but isn't this extortion? If I don't give the kids what they want, I may be in store for a not-so-nice surprise.

I feel like I am paying for protection. "Here kid, you like Twix bars? How about another Snickers?"

The kids on Halloween seem to get a free get out of jail card. Vandalism is considered just part of the trick.

What's up with the idea of giving the kids candy? Any other night if a kid asked me for candy, I would tell them to work for it.

"Hey, kid, you want some candy? Why don't you earn it? I've got a couple of weeds in my pine straw island next to the rose bushes. I'll tell you what. If you pull the weeds, I'll give you a piece of candy."

Whatever happened to the idea of kids doing some chores to earn things? Kids these days just ask and receive. If they don't get what they want, they can vandalize your property. I would appreciate a little honesty. Why don't these kids just tell the truth? "If you don't give me a piece of chocolate I will break your mailbox. It's leaning a little to the right anyhow."

Trick-or-treat just sounds better than vandalism or extortion.

Some parents aren't able to give out candy because they are both walking around with the little kids. When my sister is trick-or-treating with her kids, she does the same thing every year. She puts a big bowl of assorted candy on her front porch with a sign that says, "Please take ONE!"

Every year I tell her the same thing: "You should just put up a sign that says, 'Sorry! You must be the second kid!'" She never believes me when I tell her a few minutes later that the bowl is empty. It only takes a second for a kid to empty the entire bowl in a big pillow case, trick-or-treat bag.

What are their parents doing, you might ask? They are walking around with the little ones and standing on the sidewalk waiting as they go to the door and come back with their treat. The parents are on thank you patrol. "Susie ... did you say 'thank you' to that lady? Daddy didn't hear youuuuuuu. Go back and say thank you, Susie! If you don't say thank you, no more candy! We'll just go home!"

Sometimes, the parents actually come to the door with their kids. There are two reasons parents come to the door: either they want a piece of candy or they are curious what the inside of your house looks like.

For women who like to decorate, Halloween night is like a free Tour of Homes. It's finally a chance to see how your neighbors decorated their homes. As soon as I open the door, they are checking out my entire house. "I like the floor plan. Nice wallpaper, too, or is it faux painting? I would have never thought to put that bench in the foyer."

"Oh, you've had your kitchen remodeled since last year. I really like the new countertop!"

Actually, I have gotten some good decorating ideas on Halloween night! I think there should be some type of fair exchange. When the parents come to the door, why don't they bring me something? How about a wine cooler to get me through the night?

Halloween means that for the entire month of November and December your kids will be eating candy for breakfast and so will you! All parents forage through their kids' candy stash. As soon as my kids get home from a night of begging, we go through their candy to make sure everything is safe to eat.

This is a way for parents to secretly scope out what they plan on eating while their kids are either sleeping or at school. *I am doing my kids a favor!* I tell myself as I'm stuffing my face with miniature Snickers. Because of me, they won't be eating all of this nasty candy that is rotting their teeth.

"Darn! They only got one Mary Jane. I really like those! What's up with all the little lollipops? I gave out assorted candy bars. CHEAP neighbors!! I can't eat business cards! Why are these parents putting business cards in my kids' bags anyhow?"

Do parents really get additional business from advertising in my kids' trick-or-treat bags? There must be a better way to advertise: a billboard, a magazine, even a flyer in the mail would be more appropriate. What are parents thinking? "Here's some Skittles. Could you call me if you need your windows cleaned?" If I can't eat it, I don't want to look at it.

I am just about ready to call it a night when I see a group of teenagers get out of their car and start walking to my front door.

"If you are old enough to drive yourself to the house, maybe you're too old to play trick-or-treat," I mumble to myself.

After the familiar teenage greeting "Hey!" one of the kids in the group holds out a big bowl for me to drop the candy in.

"Hey, kid. I recognize that bowl. My sister has one just like it! Kid!!! ... COME BACK! That's my sister's Halloween bowl!"

TRICK AND TREAT!!! What a strange holiday. . . .

Does anyone want to trade a Snickers for three Mary Janes?

22

Actors

Whenever I stand in the lines at the grocery store, I see all of these celebrity magazines and tabloids with models and actors on the front covers. If the line isn't moving, I always grab one and start flipping through it. In every magazine there are always pictures of women who look like they are starving. They always have some type of headline. "Look Who's Starving! Look Who's Too Thin."

These magazines are all starting to look like save the children ads for Ethiopia. The actresses and models in the pictures look bony and thin as if they had not eaten a nutritious meal in weeks. Their arms and legs are toothpicks that are about to break. If you hug these people, you would run the risk of getting a splinter from the walking, talking toothpicks that we now refer to as our celebrities. I don't know whether to buy the magazine or place a concerned call to UNICEF.

If it weren't for the fabulous clothes draping loosely on their stick figures and the expensive accessories with designer shoes and purses, you would think these emaciated celebrities are too poor to buy some groceries.

These actresses and fashion models are the celebrity role models for young girls. Just by being in the public eye these women are thrust into the limelight and emulated by young girls who aspire to be just like them. Unfortunately, this has taken a toll on young girls and women, who view these celebrities as the ideal of what women should look like to be considered beautiful and sexy.

Our society has become a one-size-fits-all mentality: all women should be one size—very thin! The actresses are always talking about the pressure in Hollywood to be skinny to get the best parts for television and movies.

I remember watching the TV show *Ally McBeal* with Calista Flockhart. She played the lead role of Ally, an attorney for a Boston law firm. That was one of my favorite shows; it was on for five seasons starting in 1997 through 2002.

The actress Calista Flockhart, about five feet six, weighed under one hundred pounds while filming this show. Her weight loss had become visibly more noticeable from season to season. It became so distracting to watch the show as you gasped at how thin she was becoming as the show progressed from week to week.

In most episodes, they would go to the local bar after work to have a drink, listen to music, and unwind. They would show Ally dancing with her colleagues, who were also attorneys in the fictitious Boston law firm. I kept thinking, why are you dancing—sit down! Order an appetizer! Ally McBeal needs a meal! The entire female cast was super skinny. What did the director say? "I can't see your clavicle. You're too fat! We need a close up shot of a rib. What did you eat for breakfast?!!

"The oatmeal is sticking to your ribs. They won't show up on film! This was stated in your contract. *All* ... ribs ... must ... show!" the director yells with obvious frustration.

"The breakfast bar we had catered in with the hot oatmeal, brown sugar, and raisin toppings were for the staff!

"Where's my assistant?! Jenna! Didn't you put up the sign: Each actor gets one raisin—no oatmeal?!!

"I told all of you actresses: no chocolate—EVER! I don't want to see a thigh under your mini skirt. Your entire leg should be the width of your ankle! Proportion ladies ... proportion! Let's get it together!!"

What do you call one slice of pizza, a piece of lettuce, and two carrots? A Hollywood buffet. This is a feast for an entire female cast!

The production assistant can carry in the complete buffet in her purse every day for work for the entire cast. "It's lunch time, Jenna. Could you get your purse and set up the buffet!" yells the director. "And don't forget to break the lettuce leaf into eighteen pieces so everyone can have an entrée!"

In Hollywood these days, if you don't wear a size zero, you are considered fat. You can have a difficult time even finding work. Jennifer Love Hewitt was on the cover of *PEOPLE* magazine for being featured in an unflattering bikini shot. The title of her article: "Stop Calling Me Fat."

Jennifer is a size two, and she is considered fat! Research shows that the average woman in America is a size fourteen. Half of the women in this country would love to be a part of that fat farm in a size two.

Marilyn Monroe was a legendary actress and sex goddess of the '50s who defined the standard of beauty for the American woman. Marilyn was a size twelve. Can you imagine what her agent would be saying to her today. "Marilyn, you are a goddess … an icon … but you can't work because you're too fat! Stop eating until you are a size zero."

Even the models these days are skinnier than ever. In the '80s, a standard size for a model was a six or eight; now the standard size is a zero or a two—if you're borderline fat. Just think: our gorgeous supermodels of the '80s like Christy Brinkley, Cindy Crawford, and Carol Alt would be considered plus-size models today.

Let's be real; most people are not built like supermodels. Even supermodels aren't built like supermodels. Many of these models eat very little and certainly are not the epitome of exuberant health.

Just recently in the news, size zero supermodel Kate Moss was quoted as saying in an interview for the fashion website *Women's Wear Daily,* "Nothing tastes as good as skinny feels." This was Kate's response to the interviewer's question, "Do you have any mottos?"

She seems to live this credo, as her modeling career has been based on her gaunt, waif-like figure. Kate now has a clothing line that only goes from a size zero to six. I guess if you're not a size six or under, you don't deserve fashionable clothes.

I was wondering what Kate Moss might have been thinking, *You know, a potato is still a potato. You can dice it, smash it, fry it, but you can't cover up the fact that it's still big and round.*

Or, maybe not—maybe it's just me thinking what she might be thinking. Anyway. . . .

Look how most of these models appear when they stop modeling. They are about twenty to thirty pounds heavier. Why???? Because they are finally allowed to eat, and their bodies adjust to a normal weight replacing their former skeletal figures.

I recently saw a model, Filippa Hamilton, appear on the *Today* show discussing how she was fired from Ralph Lauren for being too fat. Filippa, who is only twenty-three, is five feet ten inches tall, one hundred and twenty pounds, and wears a size four. "I was too large," she tells news anchor Ann Curry. "They told my agency I was fired because I could not fit in the clothes anymore."

Hey darlin', I got news for you; ninety-nine percent of American women don't fit in those clothes anymore!

Without all the makeup, great lighting, and touched-up photos, who knows how healthy these girls would look if you saw them walking down the street? I would bet their natural look is more scary-skinny than supermodel sexy as portrayed in the touched-up magazine photos.

I always find it interesting that women's clothing sizes are based on women who are either teenagers or in their early twenties. There are a few models who always state, "I just have a high metabolism." Well, all of us had a much higher metabolism when we were nineteen!

Now, forty-year-old women are expected to fit into clothing sizes made for nineteen and twenty-year-olds. It's scary watching some of these fashion shows. *We should not have to see models on a catwalk that look like they should be modeling hospital gowns with a rolling IV pole trailing behind.*

Why are we allowing the fashion industry to define what women's bodies should look like? There are women who are wearing a size zero and the clothes are hanging on them. You know what size comes after a zero? It's a minus two.

If the fashion industry decides there is a market for minus sizes, that will be our new standard for fashion. I just can't imagine going into a store and saying to the salesperson, "You only have these pants in a size zero? I'm not that fat! Where are your minus sizes? I told you ... I wear a minus two. Why are you showing me sizes from the plus-size section in a size zero? Do I really look that obese??? Stop calling me fat!!!"

If the designers wanted to know what the clothes look like on a hanger, then they should keep the clothes on the hanger.

Why do they have models to model the clothes? Why don't they just have those revolving hangers like they do at the dry cleaners? They press a button and all the clothes circle around the store on a track.

I don't understand why we have to see the clothes on a walking hanger! The models and actors always say, "I don't have an eating problem. I just work long days and work out too much. I am so stressed from working long days that I forgot to eat."

That makes sense to me. When we have a lunch break at work and all the other people are eating, I didn't know I was supposed to eat!

Working too much and working out has nothing to do with it. It's the six hundred calorie a day diet. Oh, give me a break. The only way you will ever see any of these girls on a treadmill is if they are attached to a feeding tube. When was the last time you saw a picture of any of these girls running or working out at the gym? I have never seen a picture of Lindsay Lohan out for her daily jog. These women aren't working out. They would collapse!

There are several television shows currently in the tabloids where the media states that some of the girls are way too skinny, and they have been losing weight at an alarming rate. It seems as though when one girl in the cast goes on a diet and becomes really skinny, the other girls don't want to look like the fat actress.

It's like there is a competition. "You bitch! You're skinnier than me. I'll show you! I can starve myself better than you. If you eat two grapes, I can eat just one."

"I saw you eat that cookie. I knew you would lose!"

"Does anyone want to share this piece of celery with me? I had this left over from lunch yesterday. Just one bite a day keeps the cellulite away!"

What is their social life like? "Do you want to come over for dinner tonight? I thought we could cook spaghetti. If you're really hungry, we can boil two pieces!"

All of these models and actresses who are starving themselves look like skeletal bodies with the bobbing heads. Ethiopians are looking at them saying, "You're doing this on purpose? I'll eat your food!"

In other countries, being really thin is a sign of being poor. Not in America. You are thin by choice. That's right. You make the choice not to eat and to starve yourself on purpose. You are not thin because there is a lack of food around. There are plenty of restaurants at your convenience, including fast-food restaurants if you are really in a hurry.

Everywhere the eye can see we have grocery stores and gas stations, many having a restaurant inside. There is not only food, but an abundance of food. The more money you have and the more famous you are, the less food you want to eat. If you are wearing designer clothes in a size zero and they are falling off, then you are super rich.

Some silly people still associate money, power, prestige, and fame with making a multi-million dollar salary, living in a super big house, driving a Rolls Royce or Bentley, and traveling all over the world.

Wrong! All your answers are wrong!!!

If you can fit in a size zero, you are rich and famous! If you have the money and the fame to starve yourself on purpose, you are now part of the most powerful and elite class of Hollywood. "We'll show all those poor people. We can buy all the food we want, but no one can make us eat it!"

The poor worry about eating. The rich and famous worry about not eating. "I'm too rich to eat like those peasants! I'll show them; I'll just starve myself on purpose!"

The pictures on the front covers of the *National Enquirer* look like a new edition for *National Geographic* under the heading: "Starving Models/Actresses in America—Fully Clothed."

Our little girls and young women have been starving themselves for decades trying to be accepted in a society where the concept of beauty and femininity is created by the media, fashion, and entertainment industries.

There is so much pressure now in school and in the workplace for girls to be skinny to be accepted. It's about time for our young women to have healthy role models to look up to and emulate instead of obsessing about what size they are, and starving themselves to look like the facade of beauty defined in the magazines and on the movie screens.

The 2009 November issue of *Glamour Magazine* featured beautiful, plus-size models posing nude on the cover. The models actually looked healthy, gorgeous, and with more vitality than former emaciated cover models that leave normal women feeling deformed.

Kudos to *Glamour*! I think ads should feature regular everyday people. If the stores are doing ads for their clothing, why not have real workers who are part of everyday society wear the clothes? For instance, if Macy's needs models for their new arrivals, why not use actual Macy's employees to wear the clothes in the ads and fashion shows? Aren't these the types of people who are actually buying the clothes anyhow?

Why are the models representing fashion only for the minority of the population? The majority of the women are not a size zero, two, or four. It certainly is important to eat healthy and exercise, but we all come in different shapes and sizes. We are not a one-size-fits-all size zero society.

I think we are all ready for a new headline: "Models/Actresses in America—Healthy and Fabulous!"

By the way, does anyone want to split a raisin? I am really stuffed. I had an extra large peanut for lunch on the airplane!

23

Victoria's REAL Secret

We are all familiar with Victoria's Secret. This is the store with the women's sexy lingerie featured by longhaired, seductive, full-figured mannequins in the front windows of their stores.

When the stores were rapidly expanding to every major shopping center in the 1980s, the biggest joke was always— What is Victoria's secret? This comment was always followed by a goofy chuckle with the reply—She's a slut.

I never understood this entire comment and never got the joke. People would laugh, and I just didn't get it. Maybe my mind is just too questioning and too logical to comprehend this silly joke about a ladies' undergarment store.

I'd like to share with you a few of Victoria's secrets. Do you want to know what the real secret is? I figured this out a long time ago. The real secret is—whatever you don't have, Victoria's Secret can make you look like you do have. The whole premise of this store seems to be—we will make every part of your body that is flat look fuller. It's like, I have a secret: I don't really have boobs, but now I do! That's where the name Miracle Bra came from.

Look, it's a miracle! They must have hired a marketing genius for that one. Miracles used to be associated with momentous events, like a parting of the Red Sea. Now it's associated with boobie pads.

Even the history of Victoria's Secret in itself has been somewhat of a mystery. Victoria's Secret was actually started in San Francisco, California in 1977 by Roy Raymond, a graduate of Stanford Business School. Roy walked into a department store to buy lingerie for his wife, felt awkward, and was very embarrassed trying to pick out a gift of lingerie in such a public environment.

He realized there is an unmet market for a store where men and woman could buy lingerie in a more private and secluded setting, and opened up his first store in the Stanford Shopping Center. The store was a success and was followed by the opening of three more stores and a mail order catalogue business.

After being in business for five years, Roy sold the company to The Limited in 1982. This company has done such a great job of marketing that lingerie is now synonymous with Victoria's Secret.

Victoria's Secret now has a clothing line which features everyday and business attire: lounge wear, shoes, and swimsuits, in addition to the heavily marketed lingerie. The spokeswomen for the lingerie are gorgeous supermodels called Victoria's Secret Angels. The *Angels* are featured in their catalogues, commercials, and, of course, the highly anticipated, televised annual fashion show.

Victoria's Secret is just the kind of place Roy Raymond had in mind when he opened his first store: a store where men could feel comfortable buying gifts for the women in their lives, and women would feel comfortable purchasing lingerie for everyday wear and those romantic occasions.

Although Victoria's Secret may be the largest lingerie retailer in America, they certainly have room for additional opportunities to grow the business. I have always wondered why there is no men's line for underwear in the store. There is so much male traffic coming through the stores to buy a gift for their wives or girlfriends, or to just hang out while the woman in their life is shopping for items for herself.

This just seems like a missed opportunity to increase sales. The guys are already in the store. Why not have a men's section where they can buy underwear and loungewear for themselves? They could change the name to Victor and Victoria's Secret. One half of the store could be for "Victor's" and the other half for "Victoria's."

It seems only fair. Why should women be the only ones to benefit from padded underwear? Men need a little help looking more endowed in certain areas as well!

How about Miracle Bras with matching Miracle Briefs for the man in your life! What a great gift idea! Men are tired of the same boring socks and underwear for birthday and holiday gifts. And they are so difficult to shop for anyhow! You have a limited selection of underwear, cologne, neckties, or electric shavers … it's the same gifts every year. At least when you purchase a pair of the Miracle Briefs you will know it is something he does not already have!

When he tries them on he will be so surprised what it does for his. … He'll say, "Look honey, it's a miracle!"

It is truly amazing how many miracles happen in this store!!!

Now we could shop at Victor and Victoria's Secret and buy the Miracle Brief gift set with the matching socks. We could finally have sexy men featured in the catalogues as well. That would be the first section I will be looking at. For the gift ideas, of course!

It would certainly make the annual televised fashion show a lot more fun watching gorgeous male underwear models strutting down the runway! Why should the fashion shows only feature female models? The women want to see men in their underwear, too! The gorgeous male models could walk the catwalk with the women.

There can be male Angels, too! Just put a pair of those feathered wings on the men and let them strut down the catwalk.

Move over mannequin ladies. Make room for the mannequin men!! Let's dress up that store window!

I usually prefer to place my Victoria's Secret orders from the catalogue. I am completely confused of what to buy when I am in the store. There must be at least a hundred different styles of bras. I can't make up my mind with all the varied styles, and I don't feel like trying all the garments on in that little closet they call a dressing room. Besides, I didn't take my Magic Mirror pill this morning before I left the house.

There are full coverage, demi-shape, racer-back, push-up, padded, not padded, lightly padded, lined, underwire, T-shirt bras ... and the list goes on and on and on! At least when I order from the catalogue, I can take my time and try to figure all this stuff out. Once you figure out what style you like, then you have to determine what size you are. Who came up with the sizes for bras? I am still confused!

Where did the letters A ... B ... C ... D ... come from? Why are they grading my boobies!!! *In this bra school, an A flunks. It is better to have a C average or maybe even a dumber grade like a D.*

Victoria's Secret has their version of the Wonderbra, but how about a new line of panties called the *No Wedgie Wonderwear.* That has to be the most annoying thing ... you put on a pair of underwear in the morning and a short time later you are almost wearing a thong because of the ride up. Even though I dislike the hassle of trying on clothes in the store, I always try on the panties at Victoria's Secret because all the styles fit so differently!

I take handfuls of different styles to try on, and then I start moving around in my little dressing room to try and check how much they ride or will they actually stay in place! It would certainly save me a lot of time if they could just put a numerical rating of one to ten on each panty to determine how well they stay on your booty.

The Wonderwear could have a rating of *one* for no booty ride; and if there are panties that move around excessively, they would have a higher rating with *ten* being the worst. If the underwear were rated, I wouldn't have to spend an hour trying on a hundred different pairs and dancing around in the dressing room to see if they will go for a ride or stay put! There should be some type of lingerie law that requires panties be regulated with a numbering system for wedgies!

The food industry has the FDA. Where is our "PANTY POLICE"?

There was a story in the news in June 2008 about a California woman who is suing Victoria's Secret for a defective thong from their "Sexy Little Thing" line of panties. The lady even appeared with her lawyer on the *TODAY* show being interviewed by Meredith Vieira. This is the start of the interview as "thong lady" gave her testimony. "Meredith, I was putting on my underwear and the metal popped into my eye. It happened really quickly. I was in excruciating pain. I screamed. That's what happened."

The story went like this: When *thong lady* put on her underwear, the decorative heart-shaped pendant that was attached with two staples to the string on the side of the thong broke as the string was being stretched. "The undergarment is defective in both design and manufacture," the attorney tells Meredith. "This is a product liability case."

While putting on the thong, one of the two staples that were attached to the heart pendant flew off, had a slingshot effect, and hit the lady in her left eye, causing three cuts to her cornea, a trip to the hospital, and several missed days of work.

I do think it is very dangerous to have flying objects hit you in the eye. Aren't we always saying to our kids, "Don't do that! You could poke someone in the eye!" The *perilous panty* even got air time as it was featured on the show. It looked flawed to me— only two little staples to attach the heart-shaped pendant. C'mon now, Victoria's Secret! Panties stretch when they are put on!

This could have happened to any one of us. Women need to stick together. I could have had a chipped tooth or ended up with a flying heart carved into my face. I guess Janet Jackson isn't the only woman to have a wardrobe malfunction. I don't think I want to risk going blind to wear sexy panties.

Thong lady works for the Department of Transportation and, according to the news reports, she missed several days of work. I just can't imagine placing that call to my boss: "I can't come back to work. My sexy underwear blinded me. Hope to see you soon!"

By now, many of you are probably wondering the same thing I have been thinking. Where were the Angels? Victoria's Secret Angels should have been there for her protection during her time of need. What were they doing, you might ask? Their hair and makeup! They were too busy doing their hair and putting on makeup to assist. I bet the male Angels would have come to her rescue. This is another example of why we should have Victor's Angels.

I was just thinking, *You know, I'm lookin' for a good lawsuit, too.*

"Hey, thong lady! I want in. As I said, we women need to stick together. We could file a lawsuit together. I'll appear in court with you and testify in front of the judge."

In the courtroom, I'll say, "Your Honor, it's my underwear. I want to sue for wedgies. I am inconvenienced and I am injured. Because Victoria's Secret has not made the Wonderwear as I requested during my additional notes on my online order, I am now involuntarily wearing a thong.

"It happened really quickly. I was in excruciating pain. I screamed. That's what happened. Just like what happened to thong lady. Except my injury is not to my eye; my butt crack hurts. Your Honor, I have friction burn from that little thong string moving all day long. I need medical treatment, too!

"I missed three days of work. I couldn't sit down to drive around to my sales calls. I tried working one day, and I had one of my doctor customers take a look at my friction-burned butt. He said it could be second degree.

"In addition, Honorable Judge, I agree with thong lady's lawyer. 'The undergarment is defective in both design and manufacture.' So whatever her lawyer says goes for me, too! Ditto! Your Honor . . . Ditto!!!"

Why is there not a warning sticker for all panties for cornea abrasion or butt crack burn? Other hazardous things that I purchase have a warning sticker. Even my hair dryer has a warning sticker. "Do not use in the shower." My toothpaste has a warning on the back label. "Do not eat." These are all good reminders.

Without the warnings, I could have eaten some toothpaste as I was drying my hair in the shower. Then I would have really missed a lot of work!

Oh, those treacherous thongs. Treacherous, I say!

I'll tell you another little Victoria's Secret. Their home office is actually not in London as the catalogue states. It is really in Ohio! Columbus, that is, my former college town!

There is no Victoria, and there never was. Just sounds very European like a London address.

Kind of makes you think of Queen Victoria and her sexy little secret of her Miracle Bra and matching lace panties under her formal Royal attire.

Now ... about Santa Claus. ...

24

Happy Holidays!

I can hardly believe it is already the HOLIDAYS as the time period from Thanksgiving through New Years is now referred to. It's a nice time of year when most people are so cheerful and happy to get some time off of work and visit with family and friends.

It's a time of gift giving and gift receiving, shopping, eating, parties, and drinking! Sounds great! But for some people this can be a very stressful time of year.

There is a lot of work to be done to get ready for the holiday season! Many people travel for the holidays and have to deal with long security lines at the airport, flight delays, and traffic jams on the roads. For some people, just being around their family and their spouse's family can cause strife! Trying to find the appropriate gift (and correct sizes) for everyone on your gift list can be exhausting, stressful, and time-consuming!

Putting up all the holiday lights and holiday decorations can take hours—not to mention taking the trees and lights out of storage and untangling all the light cords! Shopping for groceries, preparing the holiday meals, cleaning up the kitchen, and doing the dishes after each meal is ... so ... much ... WORK!

Having guests in your house to visit is fun for a couple of hours, but after a day or two, you're ready to sell the house—with them in it!!! So, with all of this JOY, why do we look forward to the holidays?

It's like we have holiday amnesia and forget how stressed and exhausted we are during the "season to be jolly" and can't wait till next year to do it all over again!

Let me tell you how my holiday season is going. I don't especially like to shop. I don't like dealing with mall traffic. I don't enjoy spending hours in a shopping center just browsing until I see something that I think I should purchase.

My kids are now at the age where they are so difficult to shop for! I really had no idea what to buy them for Hanukkah! They no longer play with toys, and they already have the Wii, iPod, and all the other little handheld electronic video games ... so what else is there?

I bought them each one of those charging station organizers. I thought what a great gift! They can never find their chargers for their cell phones, iPods, and other gadgets! The gift of organization—that's what I was giving them. I thought they both would love it! No more yelling and screaming throughout the house, "Hey Mom! Have you seen the charger for my iPod?"

"Where's my cell phone charger? I thought I saw it under the couch yesterday."

"Stupid phone! Won't hold a charge for more than four hours!"

I also bought them these surround sound earpiece headphones to use while they listen to their iPods. What kid wouldn't want a home theatre version of surround sound in their ears as they listen to their favorite songs?

I absolutely loved those new technology battery-free flashlights that you just turn the crank for electrical power. What a great idea! I thought to myself, *Next time the power goes out the kids can use their flashlights!* What a fun toy for all ages, I decided. I never seem to have the right size batteries, and the few I bought were used for the flying-talking-ghost in my front yard for Halloween. I decided this toy was a surefire hit! I bought a blue one for Brandon and a red one for Morgan. Great technology and pretty colors ... how could I go wrong? They come in a variety of different colors and are easy to use. Turn the crank to charge up, then press the ON button.

They received a few other gifts: pajamas, box of See's chocolates, and a few other small items. They opened their presents and gave me a puzzled look. "Is this it?" Morgan asked as if these were the gag gifts and the real gifts were coming next.

"These aren't really our gifts?" Brandon evidently decided he was going to take charge of the questioning.

They hated EVERYTHING! Well, not entirely true. They stuffed their faces with the chocolate! At least they liked the chocolate. Chocolate is a one-size-fits-all kind of gift. I didn't have to worry if the chocolate was going to fit. I really dislike having to go to a store and exchange items for a different size.

Who knows, maybe on a subconscious level I was purchasing items that I would have liked to have!

"Where did you get this stuff?" They yelled at me in unison.

"I bought most of the gifts at Walgreens," I replied proudly!

"Walgreens? The pharmacy?" they screamed in horror.

"Well, I looked at their circular in the newspaper, and they had great prices for holiday gifts!" I replied, pleading for mercy!

Walgreens was the winner! Yes. . . . It seemed like the logical choice. It was close to my house, and I wouldn't have to deal with the crowded malls. Plus, the prices looked excellent!

I thought it was a brilliant idea!!!

Brandon was ranting and raving. . . .

"Why would I need an organizer? I'm not a businessman. I'm just a kid! The only thing I have a charger for is my phone. I charge everything on the computer!

"I don't need to organize. I have a drawer! That's where I throw stuff!

"The pajamas make me look like a clown! What kid plays with a flashlight?"

Then Morgan chimed in. "Take it back! These earbuds are too big for my ears! The stupid earpieces won't stay in!" she yelled, as she was still trying to smash the adult-size earbuds into her small ears.

"Oh well . . . sorry, Morgan. I guess I bought the wrong size," I say gently, only to be interrupted by . . .

"Take it all back!!!" they both screamed.

Brandon went to the desk in the kitchen and got the calculator. After about a minute he said, "I figured out the approximate value of all of these items, so you can just get me a gift card in this amount."

"Me too!" yelled Morgan.

That's when it hit me like a ton of bricks. This is the reason for Santa Claus!

I felt like I had just discovered the eighth Wonder of the World!

Who else can you blame bad gifts on!

This is why kids grow up with the belief in Santa Claus! This is the secret of the Gentiles!!! This is soooooo Brilliant!

Why didn't the Jews think of this? My kids know where their gifts came from. Mom went to the drug store and purchased a few things. The non-Jewish kids grow up in believing that their gifts came from a fat white-haired man in a red velvet suit whose sleigh flew over their house with a red-nosed reindeer leading the way.

Sounds believable to me!!!

This is why non-Jewish kids are taught about Santa Claus as soon as they are born! Their parents are smart. This is borderline genius! Let's get the kid to believe that someone else buys all these gifts every year!

If little Kimmy starts to cry because her new dolly won't burp and fart, her parents can just say, "I'm sorry, sweetie. Santa didn't do a good job this year! Mommy will talk to him. I'll write him a letter to complain." Little Kimmy then looks at her mommy with loving eyes knowing that she had nothing to do with the dud doll.

My kids get a gift they don't like, and I get the familiar "you're an idiot" look! I am going to start a new crusade. Jews for Santa!

I am a believer!!! Next year my house will be the one decorated with the six-foot inflatable Santa Claus in the front yard. If my kids don't like their gifts next year, I can just say, "Hey, take it up with Santa. He's in the front yard!"

Instead of leaving him some milk and cookies on Christmas Eve, I can just leave some latkes and applesauce on a plate in the grass. Maybe we can even talk him into playing a game of dreidel.

Obviously, I am totally clueless at gift giving. Maybe I would do better at gift receiving.

I usually don't receive gifts from the kids, but Morgan gave me a box of chocolates that was gift wrapped. I was so impressed!

"Oh, Morgan. That's so sweet. You got someone to drive you to the store to buy me a gift and then you wrapped it yourself!"

"No, Mommy," she said. "You paid for it! I put this in the cart when you were about to check out at the grocery store. You didn't notice because you were talking to the lady behind you!"

Then Morgan said, "The candy was already wrapped, too! All I did was take it out of the bag when we got home!"

I think this just might be the beginning of a Mintz family holiday tradition!

I decided to go outside and walk to a neighbor's front yard to have a talk with Santa. I brought him some of the leftover latkes from dinner. Santa was just sitting there in his sleigh holding the reigns, obviously still waiting for the reindeer to fly. He is so patient!

"Hey, Santa, where's Rudolf? I don't see him out in front."

"That's him, Melissa. He just got his 'nose done'—for medical reasons, of course! His new nose doesn't require any batteries; he can just turn the crank and press the ON button!"

HAPPY HOLIDAYS! . . . and don't step in any reindeer pooh.

25

Coming to a Theater Near You

I feel as though I should begin this chapter with the disclaimer they put at the end of movies. "All characters appearing in this work are fictitious. Any resemblance to real persons, living or dead, is purely coincidental."

I just can't. Why? Because . . . this is my life. . . .

"You need to go to the grocery store and buy a duster!" Brandon yelled as he came through the door, swinging his backpack off his shoulder to fly against the wall in my foyer.

"What are you talking about?" I asked, still a little confused.

"My dad is going to be here in an hour, and we are buying him one of those Swiffer dusters for his birthday. He's taking me and Morgan out to dinner."

"Why would you buy him a duster as a gift?"

"Because his apartment is dusty and he doesn't have anything to dust it with. I hate all the dust when I'm over there! Besides, I can hardly even breathe in that place!"

"Well, I'm not buying it!"

"We'll give you some money. Hey Morgan," Brandon screamed throughout the house. "Get five dollars for your half!

"Here's ten dollars, Mom," he said. "Hurry up!"

"Can't you come with me Brandon?" I pleaded. "I'm not running out and buying a gift for your dad."

"You're doing it for me, Mom, not for him. Can't you do this for your son? I've got things to do! By the way, you look really nice today. I love that sweater on you, and you don't look a day over thirty-five ... please! I'll walk Goldye!"

I rushed out to the grocery store with a five dollar bill and five singles that were so crumpled and torn, they wouldn't even completely unfold. I can always tell when I use the kids' cash. The bills don't even look like they should still be in circulation. I guarantee; all the bills marked for destruction and replacement are from my kids' underwear drawer.

As I stood there in the cleaning aisle, I started to chuckle as I realized they were getting their dad the suckiest birthday gift ever. "HA! Hahahahhahahah!" I was really starting to enjoy this. The kids never bought me a birthday gift, but I would rather have no gift than get a *dust rag*. As I looked at the dusters, I realized I only had enough money for the small dusters and no refills. I came home with the gifts. "Here, there are two dusters so you can each give your dad a birthday present."

232

For some reason this was just totally crackin' me up. I couldn't seem to stop laughing as I give them the box of dusters. It's like saying, "Happy Birthday! Now go dust!!!"

"I had time to think about it while I was at the grocery store and decided I would like to contribute after all," I finally said. Following with the same *birthday theme*, I grabbed a trash bag from under the kitchen sink. "Here Brandon, you can tell your dad it's from me."

"While I am at my dad's," he said, running out the door, "I need you to make me a haircut appointment; set up my two hours for driving practice so I can get my license in a month; clean the house so I can invite a friend over; and find my phone! I lost it somewhere in the house."

"You need to take me to the AT&T store when I get back," Morgan chimed in. "My phone broke."

Why are my kids constantly demanding that I do things? Isn't this why we have kids—so that we can delegate some of our chores to them—not the other way around? When I want my kids to do anything, I have to pay them.

"Brandon, can you walk Goldye?"

"Yeah ... five dollars for the short walk and ten dollars for the long walk."

Our parents didn't pay us to do chores; we did what we were told to do. If you ask a kid to do something nowadays, they act like you are in violation of the child labor law. "Mom, I checked, and for a kid my age we can only work fifteen minutes per day without a break. I already made you some toast for breakfast, so you have to do everything else. See, I told you to make your own toast, then maybe I could have given the bird a handful of his birdseed. As it is now, I can't do anything else until tomorrow 'cause of the child labor law thing."

Brandon did convince me that I would save money over the summer break if I stopped using the maid service to help with the house. "Hire me," he said. "I can do a better job and I'll charge you the same amount." I have no idea of his rationale of how he is saving me money, but for some reason, I decide to hire him.

Brandon cleaned the house one time and charged me the same amount the cleaning service did without even cleaning my master bedroom.

"You're fired! You're ... fired!" I yelled. "Why can't you take pride in your work? You didn't clean my bedroom or the bathroom. What am I paying you for? A real maid would have done my entire bedroom–not expect to get paid for half a house."

"Here," he said, "I found your diamond ring sitting on the nightstand in the bedroom. I thought you'd want to put it in your jewelry box."

"Stop moving the bait!!!" I yelled still exasperated over his lackluster labor.

"What ... bait??" he asked as if I have completely lost it.

"This diamond ring is actually just a cheap piece of costume jewelry. Looks real–doesn't it? And expensive! If the maid takes the ring I know she is stealing from me. I have bait all around the house, and I know where it all is. Stop moving the bait!!!"

How did I get to be an employer running my own business with two belligerent employees—MY own children! If they weren't my kids, I wouldn't hire them! I have to admit, Brandon did a good job of cleaning out the garage as part of his summer job, but he overcharged me!

At least in a normal office, if you have unsatisfied employees, you can get away from them. Your kids are there when you leave in the morning and come home in the evening. *Living with two teenagers is like boarding with your two worst employees and having constant labor and money disputes.* I keep firing them, and they're still at home demanding more money. This stuff doesn't happen with real employees.

I said, "Brandon, when you have a real job, if you want to play golf and do things with your friends, you need to use your own money."

"When I have a job, I'm not using my own money!" He said emphatically. "Then why have a job? All that money should be for me."

He was now on a roll and continued with, "I'm not going to work–ever–if I have to pay for stuff. What's the point of a job? If if didn't have a job, you would have to pay–so why am I working? I'm not working to pay for stuff I didn't pay for before I had a job. Are you crazy!! Why are you being so mean! I have a job so I can have my money to buy stuff for me, not to help pay for stuff you need to be paying for like gas, food, golf, and hanging out with my friends. That's stuff you pay for!"

"Uugggghhhh!" I decided I needed a break from Brandon.

"C'mon Morgan," I said. "I'll take you to the AT&T store. What's wrong with the phone?"

"The charger thingy broke where it fits into the phone, and when I type the space key doesn't work. I have to use a dot. It's so annoying and it makes me look dumb."

"Really, Morgan, that's horrible. I don't want you to look dumber–I mean dumb, honey. We'll get it fixed."

As we entered the phone store I asked, "So . . . where's your phone baby?"

"Uh-oh," Morgan said.

"Oh, no, Morgan! You forgot your phone, didn't you!!!!"

I realized this was one of those moments that you read about in one of those New Age type pamphlets. Popular clichés were playing in my head. "You can't control the situation you can only control how you react." "Don't let life get you down." "Don't sweat the small stuff."

I thought about it for a moment, then realized–even if I yelled at her, it doesn't change anything. I would still end up back here. I had a thirty-minute drive home where she would whine and cry and plead and bug the living crap out of me until I got in the car and came back here, tonight!!!! I might as well have a peaceful ride home.

Evidently, not texting properly is a teenage emergency that has to be rectified immediately to survive another school day.

"Okay, honey," I said sweetly, "do you want to go home and get it and come right back?" Morgan looked at me taken by surprise and braced herself at the same time for the reprimand she was sure she might endure.

"Uh … okay," she said a little timidly as if this was my witness act, and I had waited to start screaming when we got in the car with no witnesses. As soon as we were in the car, Morgan braced herself for a verbal lashing.

"Hasn't Mommy been really nice to you today?" I said, just to make sure she noticed my choice for my behavior as if I had become some spiritual saint. "I mean–really–Morgan. I am being so nice today."

We drove thirty minutes back to the store, spent an hour waiting, then we were told, "We don't fix phones here. Even if you took it somewhere else, the cost would be so much you that you might as well just buy a phone," the manager said. After an hour, Morgan still could not decide on a phone.

"What feature are you looking for in a phone?" the manager asked.

"I want a phone where I can see the entire conversation when I text, not just a few sentences."

"You want a $200 phone to text? That's ridiculous! We'll find someplace to have your phone fixed!"

In a perfect world, kids would learn "concierge speak." I could shut my eyes and visualize a stay at the St. Regis Hotel, where every request is answered with, "It would be my pleasure." Unfortunately, this is not my world. My world consists of two teenagers' constant interrogations–about EVERYTHING!

We were walking into Walmart once and Brandon said, "What are you wearing!?"

"Oh ... this ... I just washed it. I was playing with Goldye, and it was wet and rainy out. She jumped on me a few times. It's just some mud and dirt."

"What's on your top?" he continued with his interrogation.

"Oh ... that ... I washed it in the morning, but I took Spike for a walk with Goldye and he pooped on me a few times. Some of it is pee, too. A few spots are probably a mixture of the two. I knew I felt something wet and warm traveling down my shoulder. I guess I just forgot about it," I said almost apologetically.

"You aren't even dressed nice enough for Walmart!" he exclaimed. "I'm going to get my own cart so nobody will realize I am with you. Get your own cart!! You can follow behind me. You look like you don't even have a home! Also, Mom, it's so embarassing; the kids in the neighborhood always ask why you walk around with the bird on your shoulder when you walk Goldye."

"Because he shits on my head ... that's why! Would you rather me have bird poop somewhere in my hair? Anyhow Brandon, why do I have to look *runway ready* to shop through the aisles of Walmart!" I yelled as the distance between us grew bigger so that nobody could associate the crazy screaming lady with him in any way. "No one else in here looks like they'll be struttin' down the catwalk in the Walmart fashion show today!!" I yelled even louder as I watched him disappear through the maze of fruit and vegetables in the produce section.

A job interview can easily be compared to my kids' constant interrogations. "What's for dinner? Why are we having this? What's in this? When did you buy this?"

"How long were these strawberries in here?" Brandon asked as he srutinized all the fruit in the refrigerator. "I know you didn't go the the grocery store."

"How do you know? You weren't even home. I picked them up yesterday on the way home from work. You were at a friend's house, so you didn't notice."

"I wasn't at a friend's house yesterday!"

"You were somewhere, maybe you were up in your room."

"Why would I be up in my room?"

"Now I remember. You were walking the dog. Yes, I'm sure of it. You were walking Goldye."

"No!! Remember, you yelled at me yesterday for not walking Goldye? When did you really buy these strawberries?"

My kitchen is always a courtroom, and I am the one on the witness stand. "When did you buy these groceries?" Brandon asked again, as if I am secretly trying to poison him with day-old food. If anything has been in the refrigerator for more than a few days, Brandon just throws it out.

"Where's the almond milk?" I asked.

"It's old. I threw it out," Brandon said.

"The date said it was good for two more weeks."

"That's unopened!!" he yelled. "The dates are for stuff on the shelf—not opened!" he said slowly, as if he has to sit me down and tell me about how life really works. How did my kid suddenly become an expert on the world's food supply in addition to always being right about everything else in the world?

I remember now. It's when he became a TEENAGER! For people who love horror movies, this is a must see—Coming to a Theater Near You–*Teenage Terror in 3-D*. It frightens me every time I think about. This is the scariest movie I have ever seen. Just think how an audience, who doesn't know my kids, would react?

They'll be frightened out of their seats! I have already decided I want Sandra Bullock to play me. After all, the movie is based on a true story just like the *Blind Side*. She did such a great job in that movie I think she could pull it off. We are both brunettes–how difficult can it be for her to act like me? I do it everyday, and I can tell you–it's not that difficult!

Since Brandon now thinks our household food supply is poisoned, I decided to take him out to lunch to a Mexican restaurant near our house. I was craving my favorite dish there–shrimp tacos. Not just any shrimp tacos. They are very lightly fried with this yummy slaw topping and an incredible sauce–I can't even describe. Sorry, I have to break from writing now. I'll be back in an hour.

"Y'know, Brandon," I said as he was looking over the menu, "when you work here, I will be here all the time."

"Work here?"

"Yeah, remember? Steve, the owner, said when you are sixteen to come see him, and he'll hire you. Well, you'll be sixteen in a few months. So when you're working, I'll sit in your section."

"Why would you do that?"

"Because if I sit in your section, I can leave you a big tip!"

"Well, I'd rather you just leave me alone and put money in my account!!"

Okay ... I'm back now ... Do I have any sauce on my face ... anyone? ... anyone ... ?

"This is so hard. Nothing in life prepares you for this!" I groan as if I am alone on a battlefield waiting for the reinforcements that never arrive.

I think all families are dysfunctional to some degree. This has certainly been confirmed by all the "reality" shows on television. I have to admit, it is a nice validation to see other families dealing with drama and everyday family issues as well. As a matter of fact, even during my childhood I have spent most of my time pondering the **two Rs.**

Who the hell **ARE** *these people? And why* **ARE** *we living in the same house!!!*

Hallmark is missing out on a lot of business. "Where are all the cards for normal people?" I ask whenever I enter their store. "What do you mean there isn't a dysfunctional section?"

These cards are all written with dialogue from the *Lifetime* channel. I could spend an hour in there and still not find an appropriate card. This is a typical Hallmark card:

Dear Helen Sue,

Happy Birthday from Everyone!

You're just like a fine wine. You get better and more beautiful as you age.

We are ALL so very blessed to have you in our life!

Have a wonderful day!!

Love,
Susan, Dave, Linda, Betsy, Rob, Lori, Sheila, Bruce, Manny,

Over . . .

Bob, Tess, Craig, Steve and Ed

P.S. We all chipped in this year and bought you that vacation home at the beach! Surprise!!!!!

This is not how normal (like me) Americans talk. These cards are all so sugary sweet, just after reading a few of them I can feel a cavity start to form! "Dr. Harden, I know I didn't have any cavities at my cleaning last week, but I spent thirty minutes reading birthday cards at the Hallmark store, and my left molar started to hurt."

This would be a sample card from their new *dysfunctional cards* for *normal* American people:

Happy Birthday. This is your crappy card. You never get me anything for my birthday! You didn't even remember it last year ... dumbass.

P.S. Howie, you still owe me $25.00 for the hot dogs and peanuts from the Braves game.

Pay up, JERK! Those Astros really sucked!!

See you at work. DON'T BE LATE!

Somehow, I always knew I'd end up writing for Hallmark one day.

After several months of filming, *Teenage Terror in 3-D* was out in the movie theaters throughout the country. The kids and I were so excited to finally see ourselves on the big screen. We were given our 3-D glasses as we entered and found three seats together in the middle of the theater. "It's packed!" I said to the kids. "I can't believe this incredible turnout for *Teenage Terror*! This is turning out to be a very popular family movie."

The audience consisted of a mix of parents and their kids, mostly teenagers, but there were also pre-teens in attendance as well.

Once we all sat down, Morgan and Brandon started whining. "We're hungry!" I gave them money for some snacks and off they went to the concession stand.

"Are we taking a cross-country road trip?" I asked as they find their seats. "We just had lunch!"

I watched them eat their buttered popcorn, milk duds, cherry Icee, and a big box of gummy worms to share between them. "How can you still be hungry?" I asked in disbelief.

"We didn't eat this much on our seven-hour drive to Myrtle Beach! All of a sudden, the lights are turned off, and you kids broke out two hundred gummy worms and a popcorn container large enough to fit in a bathtub. They call it a tub of popcorn for a reason!"

I reached into my oversized movie purse and took out the three bottled waters that were safely hidden and gave them each one. "Here, just in case the popcorn gets stuck in your throat," I said as the previews suddenly came on.

Morgan's opening scene appeared on the movie screen.

"You suck at life!!!"

She screams at me from the back seat of the car as I'm driving. The camera moves to a closeup of me looking confused and bewildered, unsure of how to respond.

After a few moments I say, "I'm not even sure what that means, Morgan! How can I suck at life?"

We continued to watch the rest of this car scene unfold. I had a few more lines, and then the scene abruptly ended with Morgan yelling, "Don't even talk to me! Parents should be seen and not heard!!"

This was a very frightening scene. I was glued to my seat. As I looked around the theater, I noticed there are quite a few parents sitting with their teenagers. The parents looked as shocked and frightened as I did, while their kids were shaking their heads in agreement as though all parents suck at life and should be seen and not heard.

"Wow! Morgan … that performance was absolutely brilliant!" I whispered in her ear while we watched the next scene of the movie starring Goldye.

"Y'know honey," I continued, "I felt like I was actually there, re-living this entire event. The over-the-top drama and anger you showed was so realistic! My little Morgan Streep! I am so proud of you. That was just riveting! Riveting!! I'm going to call my new best friend Sandy Bullock and see about using her connections to break you into the business!"

Sandra Bullock was originally going to play me in the movie, but she backed out at the last minute. "I'm so very sorry, Melissa," she said to me during our brief phone conversation. "I'm afraid I won't be able to do it after all. I'm still fiming the Sci-Fi thriller *Gravity* with George Clooney. I just bought a Tudor-style mansion in Beverly Hills, so next time you're in town let's have lunch. You can meet my Louis!"

So, I got stuck at the last minute with tackling the most difficult job in Hollywood–playing myself.

"Awwwwww. I love this scene," I said quietly, as we watched the dinner scene with the entire family and my precious Goldye.

"We always have what Goldye wants!" Morgan yells. "Why do we have to have pizza again because 'that's what Goldye wants'?"

The kids eat their pizza and complain about their dinner. "I guess you won't eat!" I say as my standard reply to the yucky food comments.

I can tell Goldye is upset with me about her dinner, so I drive to Arby's and buy her five roast beef sandwiches from the dollar menu to mix with her dog food.

Then the movie cuts to Arby's. I am at the drive-thru window, placing Goldye's order. A voice booms out of the speaker on the outside menu. "Would you like some Arby's sauce?"

"No," I reply, "my dog doesn't care for the sauce."

"Your dog???"

"Yeah, I'm buying these sandwiches for my dog. Goldye likes your roast beef!"

"Hey y'all, the lady in the car is getting this for her dog!" yells the drive-thru cashier to the employees. "Can you believe it! She's nuts!"

"I can hear you!" I yell through the open car window. "I mix the roast beef in with her dog food! Do you want to eat the same food every day!!!" I say, hoping to prove that I'm really not the crazy lady. "Your poor dog," I continue, " I treat mine as my good friend.

"I'm not crazy!" I yell to them as I drive away. "I don't like your sandwiches! My dog does!"

"You wouldn't do this for me!" Brandon exclaims, when I walk in the kitchen with the food.

Y'know what? He's right, I thought as I watched this scene with Goldye come to an end. *I wouldn't.*

"Achooooooooo!" Brandon sneezed suddenly.

"GROSS! Brandon," I said as I felt some mucous mist on my arm.

"I need to go to the doctor!" he said.

"You're fine, Brandon. You have a cold."

"Sssssssshhhhhhhhhhhhhh!!! Watch the movie!" Morgan yelled.

"I feel like I'm dying," Brandon said. "I need to go to the doctor!"

"You want a prescription cough drop?? You have a cold. Stop whining!"

"Sssssssshhhhhhhhhhhhhh!!! Stop talking!" yelled the lady sitting behind us.

When my kids are sick they feign so many symptoms, I don't know whether to make them go to school or to call Make-A-Wish Foundation.

This is how I envisioned the phone call:

"Oh hello ... is this the person who grants wishes?"

"Yes it is! My name is Jeannie. What is your wish today?"

"Well, apparently my son has a case of runny nose, cough, and congestion. Our pediatrician Dr. Harry Butts told us that he has a case of RNCC. I know it's terminal.

"Look on your list they gave you for all the terminal diseases. I'm sure we are on the list ... M-I-N-T-Z. Haven't you ever heard of RNCC? My son says he's dying!!!

"His last request is for a seven-day cruise to the Western Caribbean. It has to be Western. Last year when he had his terminal stomach virus, they sent him on a cruise to the Eastern Caribbean. He is a walking miracle ... my boy! What dates do you have available for their December school break? I'm sure he will be okay during the holiday. He always tells me that he lives for his vacations.

"The entire family will have to go to make sure he is kept comfortable. My daughter Morgan carries the tissues. I will be laying out by the pool with him to make sure he doesn't get too much snot in the water. Snot doesn't sink ... Did you know that Jeannie? It just kinda floats around until it attaches to a swimmer's skin. I'm considered sort of a pool water consultant since my sister has her own pool with two little kids swimming in it.

"We always try to be considerate of the other passengers. Last year, I was there to make sure Brandon always used the tissue toilet seat covers. Stomach viruses can be so ... well ... you know.

"Jeannie ... Jeannie ... One last wish ... er ... request. Brandon's new respiratiory consultant said he should have a room with a balcony to breathe in some fresh sea air."

"I see. Who is his respiratory consultant?"

"Oh, a friend of my mom's in Florida. She's a smoker–she knows about cough and congestion. She's our new expert!

"Also, Jeannie ... about dinner ... We request to sit at the captain's table with the other VIPs on the ship. I didn't want to mention this, but I am a very famous writer. I have been traveling around the country on a book signing and lecture tour. Well, I guess I should tell you who I really am. I'm Melissa Mintz, the world–renowned expert on sneezing etiquette! I wrote the bestseller, *Snotty is Naughty . . . Just say GROSS!!!*

"Thanks for everything, Jeannie! If we have a good time on your Make-A-Wish Cruise, we may just send you some referrals!"

"You're not a normal mom!" I hear Brandon yell on the movie screen, and I am jolted out of my daydream. *Back to my life*, I thought as I watched the shoe scene.

While I was in my reverie, I missed the beginning of this scene, but I remember it quite well.

Morgan comes home from school, sits on the couch and says, "The soles of my shoes are coming off. See, I can pull it away from my shoe. I get water in my shoes when it rains!"

"Gosh, that really sucks!" I say.

"That's not what your supposed to say! You should say, 'I'll take you to get a new pair of shoes.'"

Then Brandon, who was sitting next to me on the loveseat said, "Yeah, a normal mom would say, 'I'm sorry, you must need a new pair of shoes. Let's go right now and buy you a new pair.'"

"You're not a normal mom!" They both yell on the movie screen.

There is some additional dialogue of the kids complaining about how they need new tennis shoes and me trying to convince them of my normalcy.

As this scene played out, I looked over at the kids who were still stuffing their faces with enough food to feed a small town in Indiana.

"Can I have a Milk Dud?" I asked, only to be ignored.

The three of us were silent as we watched the final scene of the movie. It's the continuation of my conversation with Brandon over shrimp tacos at the Mexican restaurant.

"Y'know, Brandon, when you work here, I will be here all the time."

"Work here?"

"Yeah, remember? Steve, the owner, said when you are sixteen to come see him, and he'll hire you. Well, you'll be sixteen in a few months. So when you're working, I'll sit in your section."

"Why would you do that?"

"Because if I sit in your section, I can leave you a big tip!"

"Well, I'd rather you just leave me alone and put money in my account!!" He continues, "Y'know, when I'm working and driving, I'll need you to put $100 in my account every month. I'll be driving, going places with my friends, eating out, and going through drive-thrus. I'll be hanging out at Starbucks, shopping at the mall with my friends ... I won't have the time to ask you for money all the time! I can't say, 'I'm seeing a movie and getting something for lunch, and I need a few dollars for gas too!'"

"Hence ... the job. Hence ... the ... job." I say again slowly, as if I have to sit him down and tell him about how life really works.

"I am so pleased with how this movie turned out," I said to the kids as we watched the final credits.

Credits

Brandon Mintz as Brandon

Morgan Mintz as Morgan

Melissa Mintz as Mommy, Mom, Bosslady,
Lil Mis (my rapper name)

(For anyone who even cares–My kids are not allowed to call
me Mother. I know they'll mean it derogatorily.)

Goldye Mintz as Goldye (None of my animals were harmed
during the making of this movie.)

All characters appearing in this work are real. Any
resemblance of your life to that lunatic Mintz family is purely
coincidental and unfortunate.

The End

Watching this movie in 3-D made it so realistic! *I loved how
I got to say the final line in the movie,* I thought to myself as I
stepped over the empty tubs of popcorn and candy boxes to exit
the theater. *I finally got the last word!* Life really is better at the
movies!

26

Universal Phrases

These are some of the things that I say to my kids. Feel free to borrow if you'd like to try them out. If you don't have children, you can say these things to any random kid. It's what you call universal phrases. They can work anywhere in the Universe; I guess is what that means.

Stop cussing, dammit!

Oh forget it –I'll just do it.

Where's my change? Really? That's all you have left?

Why can't I ever watch what I want to watch ... Can I have the remote now? C'mon ... please?!

Will you be seen with me in public if I promise not to talk?

Do you really like me better than your dad?

Can I have some of that candy?

Are you kidding me? I can't get that stain out!

What's that you're playing with? *When was that invented?*

It's true! I really did spend more than $20 for ALL of your gifts.

No, your friend can't come over–go over their house for a change.

Is that frozen slobber in the ice cream again? Can't you ever use a bowl?

Can I borrow some money? I'll pay you back when I get cash. You know I'm good for it!

Stop treating my car like a trash can!

Why can't you ever help carry in the groceries?

If you don't do this, don't ever ask me to do anything you want!

I feel like hitting you right now, but I know you'll call your attorney.

I'm the boss–I decide the restaurant! Can we go to the Thai restaurant?

Can you load the songs on my iPod? Okay, I'll do your laundry and your science homework.

Don't throw away the directions . . . I need them!

Why can't you ever turn off the lights?

You call this . . . clean???

No complaints! Be grateful I even cooked you dinner! Some kids only get cereal!

Nooooooo ... you can't have cereal!!!

Can't you just write your own sick note and sign my name?

What's going on in this movie? Can you explain it to me again??

Can you set up my computer and printer for me?

I don't love the dog more than you!

Can't you find a ride home?

Who wants to figure out 15% for the tip?

No, I'm not going to pay you to walk the dog.

Of course, you have to use your own money. I'm not buying it!!

You only played that Monopoly game twice, right? It's still in wrapping condition–now go find it! I'm not buying one more birthday gift!

27

School of Life

People need to learn to be childlike again. That does not mean to go into work, raise your hand and ask, "Boss, can I go potty? I have to make number two." What I mean when I say childlike is to see the world through new eyes—to change our perception—to see the world as we did when we were kids. Everything was new to us and exciting! We used to laugh and be silly and get excited about all the things to do and see.

We were excited to see new places and meet new people! When we met new playmates, we didn't judge them by how much money they had or where they lived, or what color hair they had; we just wanted to play! We laughed and played and had fun! We loved being alive and couldn't wait for tomorrow. Tomorrows were filled with the hope of a new day, new friends, new experiences, and new excitement. The world was our playground. We lived in the present. We lived for the now and enjoyed every moment.

Time seemed to move slower, as each activity had our full attention. We did not dwell on our past—our past was too short to dwell on. We did not worry about our future—our future was full of boundless possibilities. We believed that we could be anything we wanted to be; all we had to do was dream it, and we could achieve it. Somehow, as we got older, we were conditioned to believe that we should be mature and not laugh so much and not be silly. We should act like grownups and take things more seriously, worry about our future, and choose careers based on money instead of passion.

Many of us chose careers that we did not enjoy, and we became ill and diseased because of stress. The tomorrows were dreaded, as they just provided more of the same: an unsatisfying and unfulfilling routine. We have lost the balance in our lives and forgot the joy we had in just having fun. We are working harder and putting in more hours at work just to survive in a difficult economy. Somehow, the activities that we did for fun were no longer important. Fun was a once in a while activity. Fun was not associated with bringing home a paycheck. "Fun and work do not mix" became the new mantra.

It's time to wake up and remember who we really are and why we are here! No, goofy—I don't mean here, reading this book. I mean here on this planet. We are here to learn. The entire world and everything we experience is our school. We are in the *school of life* every day. There are no tardies. There are no detentions. There are only grades; and the best part is, we get to grade ourselves! Some days we get an A, and some days we get an F, except in this school F means *Feedback* not Failure. We have an opportunity to change and do better every day if we pay attention to the feedback.

This feedback is information that comes from us, from each individual mind, and it is our own personalized view of our actions, words, thoughts, and beliefs. We decide if we get an A or an F (feedback). We are here to play nice, get along, and respect each other's differences without judgment.

We are here to love and to be loved. We are here to learn that our differences are only an illusion. It is time for all of us to shift our focus from our differences to our similarities. Why can't we all see how alike we really are? Why do we choose to focus on our perceived differences?

Differences create **division** and **segregation**. Similarities create **unity** and **oneness**. We are all just people living our lives on the same planet. We are not black, white, Asian, Jewish, Christian, Muslim, short, fat, thin, tall, blond, brunette. . . . All of these labels that we give ourselves only separate us further from each other. With these labels we become isolated. When we label ourselves we become separate groups of people.

When we create this separation, we are no longer humans living our lives all sharing one planet. We become a race, a religion, a color. We become rich or poor, young or old. Without the labels we are all **ONE**.

There is no black. There is no white.

There is no Jewish. There is no Christian.

There is only one group of people—US! All of us are connected to each other whether we like it or not. We are stuck here on this planet together, and there is nothing we can do about it, so why not try to make the best of it.

It's like going on vacation with a group of people. Everyone is looking forward to a nice trip in a beautiful setting. It's an opportunity to get away, to see and experience new things, to meet new people, and hopefully develop better relationships with the people you're traveling with. Some people in the group know each other and some don't. Some of them get along and the others are fighting, bickering, and making the entire trip miserable for everyone in the group. At one time or another during the trip, almost everyone in the group was fighting and arguing. Only a few of the vacationers were making an effort for peace, and a feeble effort at that.

By the end of the vacation, the only concern of the travelers was who was right and who was wrong. It seemed as though no one was even trying to see the other person's viewpoint in any situation. There was constant stress and strained relationships as the people on the trip started to form separate groups. It stopped being a question of right or wrong, and the vacationers could not even recall why they were fighting.

This became a power struggle as each group tried to dominate the other. Who was in control—who was in charge—who had the power. … This was the predominate theme. The trip was ruined, and everyone had a miserable time. As the vacationers returned home and unpacked, they started to reflect on things they could have done differently to get along better so they could have enjoyed the wonderful amenities: the beautiful white sand of the beach; the turquoise-colored ocean; the pool bar with karaoke; the nice air-conditioned room with a balcony and ocean view. ... Everything was there for all of them to enjoy—a beautiful place, wonderful scenery, fun activities, interesting people. So why were they all miserable while they were on their trip?

If we can answer that question, then we will have our own answer as to why all of us are fighting and not getting along.

This is our trip—our incarnation on planet Earth. This is our journey of life. We have everything available to us on this planet to enjoy and have a wonderful time. We have a beautiful planet with varied topography and a diverse climate. We can enjoy the hot desert, the tropical oceans, and the snow-capped mountains. We have an abundance of fun activities like going to the beach, snow skiing on the mountain, and traveling to different parts of the world. We can play golf and tennis, and an activity that my mom has perfected—shopping! The list goes on and on and on.

Our world is full of interesting and diverse people and cultures. We think we are all so different, but maybe we are more alike than we realize. How will we know unless we take the time to learn more about each other? This knowledge may lead to understanding. This understanding may lead to peace.

If the vacationers took the time to listen to each other, understand each person's viewpoint, and learn to respect their differences, maybe they would have gotten along and really enjoyed their trip. They could have swum in the ocean, read a good book on the beach, or gone out for a seafood dinner. Instead, they were all miserable during their journey. They did not enjoy the wonderful things to do and could not appreciate their traveling companions. Let's not wait until we get back "home" to unpack and reflect on our life, or to try and figure out what we could have done differently to get along with each other. The time to figure all of these things out is while we're still on the trip. This is our chance to foster better relationships with the people we are traveling with.

We are all traveling companions here on our earth journey, so let's try to work things out and enjoy our trip. I like the beach. I like the ocean and the pool bar, too. I am not a fan of karaoke. I can't sing, but I can do a pretty good Milli Vanilli impersonation. How about you sing at the pool bar tonight, and I will lip-synch and try out some of my new dance moves? See how easy it is to compromise and get along?

We are all connected. We are connected to each other and connected to all life; this includes the plants and animals. Let's be really kind to our furry friends ... no lady ... not your husband. I'm still talking about the animals here. I have a very deep love for animals. I always have, and I always will. So, please treat our animal friends with kindness and compassion. They can't talk, but I know they would want me to tell y'all this.

All of us need to work together in PEACE to survive! If we are laughing, we can't be fighting!

Laughter is such a great stress reliever. When we laugh we feel lighter and happier. For that brief moment in time, we are not focused on stress at work, money problems, or even the morning headline news—we are completely in the present. We are able to appreciate that moment with joy and happiness.

When we laugh we are reminded to stop taking everything so seriously all the time. Why do we take ourselves so seriously? This book is a reminder that the people in our lives are funny! *The things all of us do and say are funny, ridiculous, and even absurd at times.* All of our lives are filled with nonsense.

We will all graduate from this school one day and go home. The question is: how are you going to get through school? Are you going to be the bully, the compassionate friend, the athlete, the caring teacher, the exceptional student, or the nonsense writer? Remember, you get to grade yourself. No cheating!

Homework for all students: Do something nice for someone every day. Even if it's just a smile or opening a door for someone. One kind act will encourage another person to do a kind act for someone else.

It does not take any more time to perform an act of kindness. If you are going through the door, how much longer would it take to hold it open for the person walking in front of you or to keep it open for the person following behind? How long does a smile take or a friendly "Hello" as you pass someone on the street?

Would it really take that much longer to let the driver changing lanes to merge in front of your car? Next time you see me driving, please let me in? I'll give you my best parade wave so you will know it is me. As a courtesy, I will respond in kind to a fellow driver and let them in front of me as well.

We seem to use time as an excuse in our lives for not doing the things that we should. "I just don't have the time!" We have all said it before. Time is what we do have. *We have the same amount of time for love, compassion, and kindness that we have for hate, evil, and destruction.* It is the same TIME. We choose how we spend our time in every moment of our lives.

In the same way, it doesn't take any more time out of your day to be playful and laugh than it does to be overly serious and stressed. The only time involved for both is a conscious choice of how you will react to life and life's circumstances.

All right, you have been very patient. You can go potty now, but go quick—we have show-and-tell.

Also, a courtesy flush would be very much appreciated!

Hey class . . . ARE YOU READY?

Let's change the world!

Let's bring laughter back!

How can I die? I'm booked.

—*George Burns*

I am going to start with a George Burns quote and finish with a George Burns quote.

Why? Because I can.

As my grandma Goldye used to say, "'Why' is a crooked letter."

PEACE

Love and Laughter